HALL of Mirrors

Confirmation and Presentist Biases

in Continuing Accounts of the

Ruby McCollum Story

Second Edition

C. Arthur Ellis, Jr., PhD

Hall of Mirrors: The Historical Context of René Descartes' Contribution to Physiological Psychology

 Gadfly Publishing, LLC ▪ Lutz, Florida

Cover photography is a hall of mirrors in the St. Louis City Museum, originally posted to www.flickr.com. Cover design by Subhash Devatwal, Pakistan. Portrait of Ruby McCollum and Dr. C. LeRoy Adams Jr. by Chinese artist collective under artistic direction of Min Zhang, China. Copyright held by C. Arthur Ellis, Jr.

Letters from Ruby McCollum and Edith Park courtesy William B. Huie Collection, Ohio State University at Columbus.

Publisher's Cataloging-in-Publication data

Names: Ellis, C. Arthur, Jr., author.
Title: Hall of mirrors: confirmation and presentist biases in continuing accounts of the Ruby McCollum story, second edition / by C. Arthur Ellis, Jr., Ph.D.
Description: Includes bibliographical references. | Dalton, GA: Gadfly Publishing, LLC, 2023.
Identifiers: LCCN: 2023907426 | ISBN: 978-0-578-84814-3
Subjects: LCSH McCollum, Ruby, approximately 1915---Trials, litigation, etc. | Trials (Murder)--Florida--Live Oak. | African American women--Civil rights--Southern States--History. | Southern States--Social conditions. | BISAC TRUE CRIME / Historical | HISTORY / United States / 20th Century | HISTORY / United States / State & Local / South (AL, AR, FL, GA, KY, LA, MS, NC, SC,TN, VA,WV)
Classification: LCC KF224.M356.E55 2023 | DDC 305.896073075--dc23

I suspect that two ruthless individuals met and tangled in Ruby and Dr. Adams.
Perhaps "egotistical" is a better word, or does it add up to the same thing?

--Zora Neale Hurston, in letter to William Bradford Huie, May 14, 1954

TABLE OF CONTENTS

PREFACE

I began my research into the Ruby McCollum murder trial decades ago to refute the writings of many scholars maintaining that she was not allowed to testify in her own defense. After all, I knew the story firsthand, because I lived in Live Oak where it happened. Aside from being aware of the trial, I was delivered by Dr. Adams in the front bedroom of our home, which was next door to the McCollums.

Eventually, I found two versions of the trial transcript—one wire recorded and one shorthand. Then I published a blended version as *State of Florida vs. Ruby McCollum, Defendant*, which documented her testimony during her trial.

I then wrote *Zora Hurston and the Strange Case of Ruby McCollum*, telling McCollum's story beginning with Hurston's reporting of the trial and then through the voice of an omniscient narrator to tell McCollum's story leading up to the trial. Much of the narrative was from my own personal recollection or the first-person accounts of my fellow townspeople.

Recently, I published *Caught Between Two Guns: The True Crime Story of Ruby McCollum*, the same story as the Zora Hurston book, with a new Preface and Afterword. The second version of the book is my attempt to frame the story more accurately, as well as to more clearly define the character and motives of Ruby McCollum after reading her letters from jail as well as other primary sources from her contemporaries.

I now find myself trying to shatter a metaphorical hall of mirrors that was constructed by various authors and film producers to present very different versions of Ruby McCollum's story, which archival history simply does not support.

Ironically, I have often felt that I contributed to the problem in writing *Zora Hurston and the Strange Case of Ruby McCollum*. After all, there was no continuous narrative of the story until I wrote that book, and there were no references to Zora Hurston and "paramour rights" until I attributed that term to Zora Hurston, the fictional character in my book. The real Zora Hurston never coined the term, but she did write about the practice of white men subjugating black women in the Jim Crow South. I simply gave the practice a convenient label.

I was caught off guard when many people cited Hurston's writings as the source of the term "paramour rights" to the extent that citations ended up in more than one dissertation. Indeed, one college professor, who produced an early documentary on the story, argued with me, insisting that Hurston did indeed use the term "paramour rights." Failing to cite her source, her final argument was that her mother had told her about Zora Hurston and paramour rights—hardly a scholarly source.

I understand that revision is a part of writing history. Historians are constantly revising accounts as new facts come to light, disproving what was once believed to be true about a historical event.

But this is not the case in revisionist accounts of Ruby McCollum's story. In fact, I find that most of these accounts either ignore archival facts or else cherry-pick just those facts that support a particular point of view—over the course of time, Ruby has become, as Thulani Davis named her stage play, "Everybody's Ruby."

Many of these accounts promise to get at the "truth" of the story, with the "truth" being simply the writer's opinion. I call this "tweeting history," since all that is added are personal hashtags, *not* archival facts. The most frequent hashtags are #rubywasraped, or #rubywasinnocent.

Then I began to ask myself, "Why?" Why would someone want to stray from the facts and re-write history?

In *Revisionist History,* Marnie Hughes-Warrington explores this very question and concludes that of all the reasons why writers are driven to revise history, a frequent one is "to make those in the present aware of poor ethical treatment of individuals and groups in the past."[1]

Unfortunately, to create a suitable setting for their versions of the story and make those in the present aware of the abuse of Ruby McCollum in particular, many scholars have ignored historical context in favor of lobotomizing her to create a generic "colored woman." It is this generic, defenseless colored woman whom these academicians then employ to tell their story in an altered historical context.

I can assert unequivocally that the Ruby McCollum I remember is *not* the Ruby McCollum of recent revisionist attempts to tell her story. Ruby was a far more complex individual—which is what makes her dilemma so much more interesting than the *To Kill a Mockingbird* take on it that many glom onto as their own "personal truth."

The Dutch psychologist Nico Frijda understood the power of persuasion gained by this technique of portraying personal opinions and beliefs as "facts" and "truth." He explained this common fallacy through the "law of apparent reality," which states that emotions are primarily triggered by events that are evaluated as real.[2] Because of this tendency, an audience watching a movie about Ruby McCollum is less likely to experience the same heightened emotional response than if it watched a documentary that claimed to be based on fact.

If this were not bad enough, the filmmakers produce what plays well to the audience, rather than what is historically accurate. Indeed, producers of documentaries are notorious for editing out facts that break the flow of their scripted narrative, as I discovered when I accepted an invitation to appear in an episode of *A Crime to Remember* on the Discovery Channel. In that episode, *The Shot Doctor,* I was shocked to see how many of my caveats were edited out. In retrospect, the producers clearly had an agenda.

Marc C. Carnes, historian and professor at Barnard College, explores this movie-industry mentality and writes, "Hollywood regards history as an inexhaustible gold mine." But although history sells, Carnes maintains that "real history is less fun than reel history."[3] As an example, he relates that when Daryl F. Zanuck took criticism for making things up in his movie *The Longest Day* (1962), Zanuck shot back, "Anything changed was an asset to the film. There is nothing duller on the screen than being accurate but not dramatic."

Revisionists accomplish this scripting of historical settings and characters to achieve their personal or dramatic goals primarily by using two revisionist tactics: *presentist bias* and *confirmation bias*, with the latter being the most prevalent kind of bias found in the Ruby McCollum story.

Presentist bias attempts to apply contemporary values and beliefs to events that happened in the past. One example of presentist bias is when readers of the Ruby McCollum story ask why she did not approach the police for protection against both the domestic abuse of her husband and the abuse of her paramour, ignoring the history of the Jim Crow South when a woman, and especially an African American woman, had no recourse in the law for being abused by a man.

On the other hand, confirmation bias—the bias most frequently brought to the retelling of the Ruby McCollum story—recalls the Mirror of Erised, a wondrous piece of magic in J. K. Rowling's *Harry Potter and the Sorcerer's Stone*. According to Albus Dumbledore, Hogwarts's school headmaster, the enchanted mirror reflects not the true image of the beholder, but the image of the "deepest, most desperate desire of our hearts." In fact, the very name "Erised" is the mirror image of the word "desire."[4]

This monograph is my attempt to place Ruby McCollum's plight into its proper historical context to confront instances of presentist bias, as well as to address confirmation bias and issue a challenge to those who metaphorically stand in a hall of mirrors of Erised. My challenge to them is to examine, objectively and without flinching, those deepest, most desperate desires of their own hearts.

Hopefully, challenging these subjective "truths" with facts will shatter that hall of mirrors that reaches back in history to reflect cherry-picked facts to support foregone conclusions and personal "truths."

Technical Notes

1. I have made every effort to corroborate citations from William Huie's *Ruby McCollum: Woman in the Suwannee Jail*. Much of what he writes about the principals in the story was corroborated by my father, who worked with Edith Park, Adams's nurse, and nurse anesthetist at the Suwannee County Hospital; physicians at the hospital; other nurses and laboratory technicians; and Thelma Curry, who started work at the hospital in the "colored" wing after Adams was murdered. There are also my memories of many of the details of the story and the trial,

including memories of all the principal characters. I carefully verified archival records in the Huie Collection in the Thompson Library at the Ohio State University in Columbus, Ohio; property records in the Suwannee County Clerk of the Court's office; the Florida Collection at the Smathers Library at the University of Florida; and records on file in the Florida State Archives and Florida Supreme Court Library in Tallahassee. I found no discrepancies of any significance in his work.

2. Throughout this text, the word "jook" is favored over "juke." The earliest definition of "jook" that I can find in the literature appears in Zora Neale Hurston's essay "Characteristics of Negro Expression," published in 1934, where she defines it as "a word for a Negro pleasure house. It may mean a bawdy house. It may mean the house set apart on public works where the men and women dance, drink, and gamble. Often, it is a combination of all these."[5]

3. No space is devoted to proving that Adams was a sociopath, since William Huie documented Adams's history of shorting cash registers in part-time jobs when he was a student, forging his letters of recommendation, falsifying billings to Blue Cross and Blue Shield of Florida and the US Veterans Administration, supplying his uncle Claude with drugs to acquire the family farm, and burning his first business for the insurance money. There are also the letters of Edith Park in Appendix A, indicating that Adams purposely killed dogs by veering off the road to hit them with his car, and the well-circulated forged will that Adams crafted to acquire the Blue Lodge. Edith Park attests in no uncertain terms to Adams's abuse of his women. Also, my father, Clyde Ellis, saw him knock Dr. Sims unconscious in the hallway of the Suwannee County hospital a day before the murder, after McCollum tried to speak with Adams in the operating room.

4. All the extant letters written by Zora Neale Hurston are archived in the Smathers Library at the University of Florida in Gainesville. For ease of access, I refer to Karla Kaplan's excellent edited compilation in *Zora Neale Hurston: A Life in Letters*. I also corroborated her version of Hurston's letters that I have cited with the originals in the archives and found no significant discrepancies.

PART I:
THE HISTORICAL CONTEXT

CHAPTER 1:

THE ROLE OF WOMEN IN THE 1950S

According to Michelle LeBaron, "Cultural messages, simply, are what everyone in a group knows that outsiders do not know."[6]

It is apparent that the Jim Crow South of the 1950s—viewed through the rearview mirror of the 21st century culture of global travel, cable TV, computers, AI, cell phones, the Internet, and social media—makes people today feel that they are "outsiders" to that culture. Because of this, it is important, especially for readers born after the 1950s, to place the Ruby McCollum story in its proper historical context.

The following circumstances are only a few examples of the role that women in this country, regardless of race, were expected to play according to the culture in the 1950s.

1. In the 1950s, abortion was illegal nationwide. If a woman became pregnant, she had no legal recourse to terminate the pregnancy. Women of means had a "D and C" for "irregular menses," or, if later in their term, took a "vacation" or visited relatives to have their abortion. A woman who lacked the financial resources to pay discreetly for her abortion and tried to abort the fetus by herself often met with disastrous consequences.

2. In Florida, when this story took place, a woman whose husband died without leaving a will could elect to receive a child's share of her husband's estate. If, for example, she had nine children, she was entitled to only one-tenth of her husband's estate, which left her dependent on the goodwill of her children.

3. In newspaper society columns, a woman was referred to by her husband's name. In the March 14, 1952, issue of the *Suwannee Democrat*, for example, a bridge party thrown by Mrs. Florrie Lee Adams, Dr. Adams's wife, and their married daughter, Laverne Jernigan, was announced: "Mrs. W. M. Jernigan entertained the Tuesday Bridge Club at the home of her mother, Mrs. C. LeRoy Adams, Tuesday afternoon."[6] The announcement continued: "Club members playing were Mrs. Alvin Brown, Mrs. Keith Wilson, Mrs. Ben Gilmore, Mrs. George Dale, Mrs. Joe Jacobs, Mrs. Bob Williams, and Mrs. C. T. Baisden, Jr. Mrs. Lee Ledbetter was a guest of the club."

4. If Mrs. John Smith divorced her husband, she practically lost her identity. She was also shunned in society for failing in her responsibility to please her husband. Adding insult to injury, her ex-husband's next wife became the new "Mrs. John Smith."

5. The Gospel of Paul in 1 *Timothy* 2:12-14 was preached in the pulpits, admonishing women to be subservient to their husbands. Women were told that their husband was the head of the household, for God created Eve as Adam's "helpmate." For this reason, Paul wrote, "I do not permit a woman to teach or to have authority over a man. She must be quiet. For Adam was not deceived, but the woman was deceived and transgressed."

6. Acts of family violence were considered a private matter and a man's prerogative. There were no laws on the books to be enforced against the male head of the household who beat his wife into submission. Moreover, the wife was expected to bear her pain in silence and accept her punishment for failing to please her husband.

7. Women who displeased their husbands were considered "evil." For example, a 1952 article in *Jet* magazine asked, "Can Surgery Cure Evil Women?" The surgery in question was a prefrontal lobotomy, which was reported as the preferred treatment for women whose husbands considered them to be disobedient. The reporter who wrote the article interviewed a grateful minister whose wife became a "happy, respected helpmate for her husband" after she had the surgery.[7]

8. "Hysteria," introduced by the ancient Greeks and further refined by Charcot and Freud in the 1800s to explain neurotic behavior in women, was still a term accepted by the medical profession in the 1950s. The origin of the word referred to a woman's uterus, which was considered the organ that contributed to female mental disorders. It was not until 1980, with the publication of the *DSM-III,* that the American Psychiatric Association officially changed the diagnosis of "hysterical neurosis, conversion type" to "conversion disorder," which applied as much to men as to women. Further, the definition of conversion disorder in that edition covered a host of symptoms for which physicians could find no organic cause.

9. The average female worker earned 63.9 percent of a male worker's salary in 1952.[8]

10. In 1952, of ninety-six senators from the forty-eight states, only one was a woman. Of the 435 members of the House of Representatives, only 9 were women.

11. Women were less likely than men to attend college. According to statistics published by the U.S. Department of Commerce on October 22, 1953, "Only about one-half as many women as men 20 to 24 years old were attending school in October 1952, and about one-fourth as many women as men 25 to 34 years of age were enrolled."[9] This represents the college-age population. And when women did go to college, they usually attended state-supported women's colleges to train as schoolteachers. Meanwhile, men attended universities with overwhelmingly male student populations, to enter the higher-paying professions of engineering, medicine, business, accounting, and law.

12. Rape laws favored men, and women were seen as enticing a man to rape them by their actions, manner of dress, or both. Women who were raped seldom came forward, since they knew they would be humiliated and blamed, becoming a victim for the second time.

13. While each state differed in miscegenation laws dictating who a woman could marry (even if she were pregnant), Article XVI, Section 24, of the Florida Constitution of 1885—which was still in the Florida Constitution in 1952—stated, "All marriages between a white person and a Negro, or between a white person and a person of Negro descent to the fourth generation inclusive, are hereby forever prohibited."[10]

The Role of Women of Color in the 1950s

In addition to the foregoing restrictions on women in general, women of color who traveled with their families in the 1950s were subject to Jim Crow laws forbidding them from entering any sort of white establishment except through the rear door to perform menial tasks. This included restaurants, grocery stores, clothing stores, and "five-and-ten-cent" stores such as Van Priest's, Woolworth's, and McCrory's—scaled-down predecessors of today's Walmart and Target superstores.

In small towns like Live Oak, there were no "colored" ends of lunch counters in drug stores, restaurants, or department stores since space did not permit.

Coloreds were not allowed in white churches. Courtrooms and movie theaters had colored balconies with separate entrances. Suwannee County Hospital had a colored wing, with no private rooms such as were available to whites who could afford them. Elective surgery for colored patients was scheduled on separate days from surgery for white patients so that the surgical instruments could be separately autoclaved. Colored people in Live Oak who could afford automobiles were expected not to drive through white neighborhoods. Instead, they had to follow the unpaved back roads through the colored quarters to reach "Colored Hill" on the edge of downtown, where they could shop and eat "among their own kind."

In 1952, Live Oak had no drinking fountains in public buildings, but when they were installed just before integration, there were separate fountains for coloreds.

Public parks and swimming pools for families were "separate but equal." No colored people were allowed in recreational areas used by whites. In a recent interview with a gentleman of color from my hometown of Live Oak, he recounted how he, at the age of 6, naively jumped into a whites-only swimming pool only to have the other children scream and run to the showers to scrub off any contamination that he might have introduced into the water.

Florida's stand on segregation was reiterated on April 5, 1957, when the state legislature passed Resolution 174, objecting to the U.S. Supreme Court ruling on *Brown v. Board of Education,* on the grounds that it "usurped" the state's power. The resolution did not carry the power of law since Governor LeRoy Collins refused to sign the resolution, choosing instead to scrawl a note over the signature area, stating that he had reviewed it but did not agree. His impassioned statement reads, in part, "If history judges me right this day, I want it known that I did my best to avert this blot. If I am judged wrong, then here in my own handwriting, and over my signature is the proof of guilt to support my conviction."[11]

When women of color planned a vacation with their families in Florida or any other segregationist state, they had to refer to the Green's book for the *"Negra Motorist"* navigating the road while their husbands drove and stopped at only the designated places they could eat and lodge in the colored community.

And, of course, McDonald's, Kentucky Fried Chicken, Burger King, Wendy's, and the like did not exist in 1952, since the concept of drive-through restaurants was only just being pioneered in a very few places in the country.

The quotation toward the bottom of the *Green Book* cover, "Travel is fatal to prejudice," is from Mark Twain's, *Innocents Abroad:*

> Travel is fatal to prejudice, bigotry, and narrow-mindedness, and many of our people
> need it sorely on these accounts. Broad, wholesome, charitable views of men and things
> cannot be acquired by vegetating in one little corner of the earth all one's lifetime."[12]

It is difficult for people today to conceive of traveling without places to eat, shop for food, go to the bathroom, or sleep—a dilemma that faced African Americans in the Jim Crow South, especially when they traveled through rural areas of the country, where facilities for both whites and coloreds were limited.

When Zora Hurston traveled to Live Oak to cover the trial of Ruby McCollum, she sat in the back of a Greyhound bus and stayed with friends of the McCollums. She ate her meals with either friends of the family or in one of Sam's jooks. Her local travel was in colored taxicabs or on foot, and when she attended the murder trial, she sat in the colored balcony and drank from a dipper in a bucket of ice water reserved for coloreds.

Figure 1: The Negra Motorist Green Book, 1949 edition, by Victor H. Green.

The Self-Image of Women of Color in the 1950s

Aside from the difficulties encountered while traveling, women of color had a tough enough time just living inside their own skins—literally.

Societal disdain for dark skin compared to light skin in the United States during the time of the Ruby McCollum story, and for over a decade thereafter, is chronicled by ads appearing in African American magazines, including *Ebony,* as well as in newspapers such as the *Pittsburgh Courier.*

One full-page ad for beauty products in the 1950s included Dr. Palmer's Skin Whitener (upper left), with the motto "Be lighter, be lovelier, be loved." The ad on the upper right for Dr. Palmer's skin whitener maintains, "Nicer things happen with brighter, clearer skin!" (Note: African Americans often use "bright" to refer to light-skinned individuals.) Another skin-lightening cream ad (lower left) claims, "He never came near me until I discovered Nadinola." The ad in the lower right gives a dramatic demonstration of the "whitening" action of the Paris Imperial product, promising "3 shades lighter in 3 days."

Ironically, the Dr. Palmer line of skin creams was and still is manufactured in the Sunshine State, where Caucasians flock to the beaches to baste themselves in tanning oil and bake in the sun until they acquire a prized "bronze" skin tone.

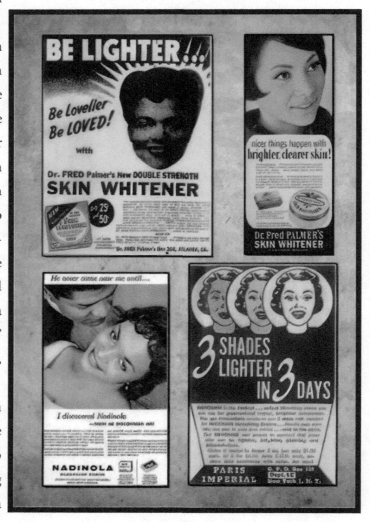

*Figure 2: 1950s skin lightening ads in Ebony
and they acquire a prized "bronze" skin tone.*

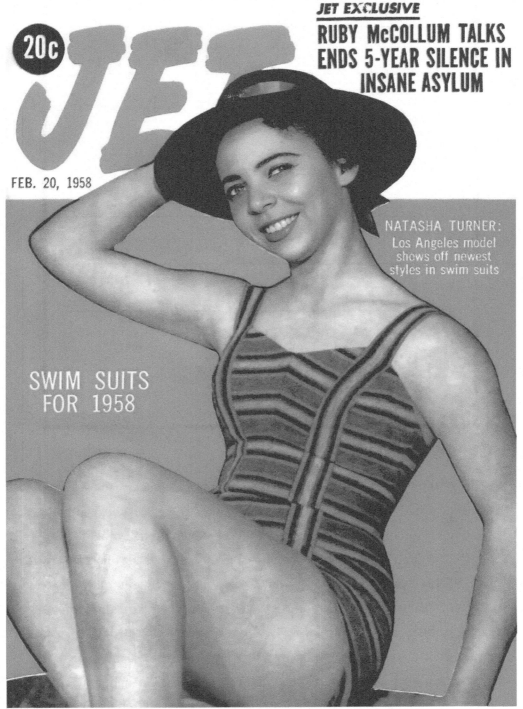

Figure 3: Swim suit model on Jet Cover, February 20, 1958.

The skin tone of the LA swimsuit model on the cover of *Jet* in 1952 clearly sets the standard of beauty to which women of color were held by the nation's trendsetters.

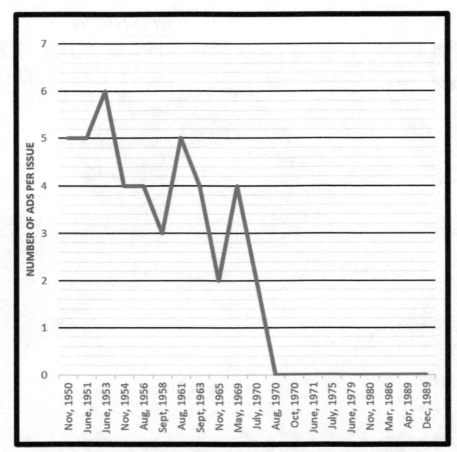

Figure 4: Frequency of Skin Lightener Ads by Date in Ebony.

The prevalence of skin-whitening creams, and their popularity by date, can be seen in a survey of the frequency of ads appearing in a sampling of *Ebony* over time. The graph above contains data collected from early, mid-, and late 1950s, 1960s, 1970s, and 1980s. Only ads with the words "bright(er)," "light(er)," "bleach," "white(r)," or "fairer" were included in the count. Ads for skin creams claiming to bleach and fade freckles or age spots, to even the skin's tone, to make it "glow" by removing "dark spots," or to "clean," "moisten," or "smooth" skin were not included. Skin-whitening creams were removed from the market in 1974 after the FDA banned the inclusion of mercury as their active ingredient, but the ads actually disappeared in 1970, four years before the ban.[13]

Also, after the 1974-89 period reported in the above graph, skin-lightening products were still available because the manufacturers switched from mercury to hydroquinone as the active skin-bleaching ingredient.

Although a causal connection is impossible to establish, paralleling the declining numbers of ads for skin-bleaching creams from the late 1960s onward is the rise in "black is beautiful" copy in advertisements, and more natural hairstyles, such as the Afro.

Beginning in the early 1970s, bleaching skin to appear whiter evidently did not market well, so claims of "lighter" or "brighter" skin gave way to the promise of "even" skin tone, free of "dark spots" or "freckles" to achieve a "golden look."

Figure 5: Before and after application of Whitenicious.

Regarding the long-term trend in skin color, contemporary reaction to skin-lightening creams in the United States is reported in *Ebony*'s Web site, "Entertainment and Culture," in January 2014.[14] In that issue, *Ebony* interviewed pop star Dencia, who had just released her "Whitenicious" skin cream. Dencia is quoted as saying that "her product is not a skin bleach—and that African Americans are the ones rushing to buy it."

The *Ebony* reporter then asks:

But do you understand people's response to the pictures? Because many people have become aware that skin bleaching is a big phenomenon around the world, particularly in West Africa where you're from. And so then we see a picture of you or a few pictures of you where you look browner and then we see this new picture of you, and not just that it's a picture of you per se, but an advertisement for a product called Whetenicious. And then it says, "Say goodbye to pigmentation and spots forever."

The reporter persists, "Is dark skin an obstacle?"

Dencia replies, "No. Dark skin is beautiful," reflecting the phrase "Black is beautiful" which was coined at the time. And then she reframes the question to speak about evening one's skin tone, the way that ads in *Ebony* did beginning in the late 1960s.

After the pop star evades the question several more times, the reporter corners her with "Your product is called Whitenicious, of course people will buy it because they want to bleach." Dencia replies, "Ok. Will Whitenicious bleach your skin if you use it on all your skin? Yes, it will."

The current West African phenomenon of skin bleaching referred to by the *Ebony* reporter is quantified in a World Health Organization report, "Mercury in Skin Lightening Products." According to the report, 77 percent of the women of Nigeria used such products in 2011.[15] Dencia, herself, was from West Africa.

In addition to skin-lightening products, 1950s *Ebony* issues carried ads for chemical hair-straightening products. These ads, featuring models with Caucasian hairstyles, guaranteed "softer, straighter, silkier" hair without the "kinky, fuzzy" hair characteristic of African Americans. The add shown at the top of the page to the right maintains that its product "helps hair grow more attractive, smoother, longer, and healthier looking," and features a model with long, soft, flowing hair befitting a Caucasian movie star.

The ad on the lower left of the page features an entire African American family with Caucasian-inspired hairstyles and the caption, "Straight hair is a family affair with Silky Strate."

Figure 6: Ebony Hair Straightener Ads

The November 1965 issue of *Ebony* addresses the topic of natural hairstyles versus Caucasian-style wigs, in an article titled "Instant Hair."[16]

Figure 7: Ebony ad for wigs, 1965

C. Arthur Ellis, Jr.

Following the downward trend of skin whiteners in the 1970s shown in Figure 4, the June 1971 issue of *Ebony* ran a pictorial article titled "Ancient African Look Becomes 'New Look' in Paris," abandoning wigs and elevating a natural, native African series of hairstyles to Parisian haute coiffure. The article features Josepha, a native of Martinique, who founded the first African beauty center in the Latin Quarter of Paris, where she employed African standards of dress, hairstyling, and cosmetics.[17]

The pride in being an African American woman with straight hair and light skin in the 1940s, '50s and '60s clearly gave way to pride in being an African American woman with natural skin and hair in the 1970s and thereafter.

It is not within the context of present-day values and notions of female beauty, but within this very real, very *different* context of the 1950s, that Ruby McCollum can be understood, not only as a member of her race but also as a member of her gender.

The Self-Image of Ruby McCollum in the 1950s

Lois Brown Miller, one of Ruby McCollum's schoolmates at Fessenden Academy, recalls her as "very reserved" and remembers other classmates describing her as "She's like selfish. She's conceited, to herself."[18]

Ruby McCollum's African American attorney, family friend, and business associate described her as "proud" and "ambitious."[19]

McCollum was also known to dress well, drive a new car, and live in the finest home in the "colored" quarters, surrounded by eight of the family's rental houses and five of its vacant lots. The McCollums also owned two working farms, one in Suwannee County and one in Marion County, with the Suwannee County farm having the largest government-granted tobacco allotment in the county.[20] Sam McCollum's farms also had plantation-style quail-hunting grounds, where he kept his expensive purebred bird dogs.[21]

Despite her pride in being wealthy and living in luxury, Ruby McCollum exhibited numerous behaviors indicating that she was *not* proud of her skin color—that it was a constant reminder that she could not rise to the top of the social ladder.

Her alternative was to live in a world of "whiteness," as readers of *Ebony* were encouraged to do by ads for skin-bleaching creams, Caucasian hairstyles and wigs, and pictures of light-skinned models living the good life.

Ruby McCollum lived in a time and place where black was not considered beautiful, and it was not until I had the chance to take a good look around her home, while attending the auction of the McCollum estate in 1954, that I saw a jar of Dr. Palmer's skin-whitening cream on her dresser. Though I had no real idea of what such a product was, the image of that jar kept coming back to me as I researched her story.

It was only recently, while looking through copies of *Ebony*, that I realized what the product was used for. I also began to realize that Ruby McCollum, like so many women of color of the time, was not comfortable with the color of her skin. In fact, she exhibited the following behaviors that revealed her dissatisfaction with her race, and her desire to transcend it:

1. Avery Trawick testified during the trial that on the day of the murder, McCollum passed in front of the patients seated in the "colored" waiting room, to confront Adams in a "white" treatment room before he led her into a colored treatment room.[22] No other colored patient would have dared enter a white treatment room, much less confront Adams for any reason.

2. According to trial testimony, on the day of the murder, as was her usual practice, McCollum drove along highway 90, which led past the front entrance of the Suwannee County Hospital and through a white neighborhood, before turning onto Ammons Avenue and then onto Sixth Street a block later to reach her home another block away on Woods Avenue.[23] Universally, the few colored people who could afford automobiles avoided this route and drove along Sixth Street from downtown, behind the hospital's colored wing at the back of the building, through the colored quarters and by Sam McCollum's jooks.

3. A nurse in the Brewster Hospital mental ward noted, "She carried pictures of this little white child with her all the time, kept 'em under her pillow, and she'd insist that we look at 'em almost every day."[24] The nurse added that the only photos she carried were those of Loretta, and that she seldom spoke of her other (black) children.

4. McCollum chose a white paramour in Adams and bragged to her attorney, "I pick my men off the top! Black or white, I get the Big Men!"[25]

5. In a letter dated December 8, 1953, and posted from the Suwannee County Jail, McCollum wrote:

Mr. Cannon, Crews

Your service is no longer needed on my case. Please send me your resignation at once also a refund of my $3000.00.

　　Very truly,
　　Ruby McCollum

P.S. I'm not loose. To deprive me of my 3 mo. Baby is murder. You promised me a new trial. I have never ran after men for my living. I was happily married. No one knows anything about me except I am Ruby regardless to color. Some one else has my case.[26]

　After taking control of her legal representation by firing her lawyer, McCollum asserts, "No one knows anything about me except I am Ruby regardless to color." This is a strong indication that she believed that she had transcended the color barrier and could demand respect, "regardless to color."

6. Ruby McCollum's disdain for men of color is evident in Zora Hurston's account of a man's remark in a local café on "colored hill": "She wouldn't even wipe her feet on nobody like us. If she had to have herself an outside man, she could'a got any kind she wanted right inside her own race."[27]

7. According to Releford McGriff, McCollum's colored attorney, Sam McCollum's affairs with lighter-skinned women were a source of irritation to his wife:

　　With her position in that community—rich, educated, 'better'n other folks,' uppity, proud—she was in a pore position to have her husband havin' them hot, high-yellow schoolteachers who were even better educated than Ruby.[28]

8. Ruby McCollum believed that her husband's employees were beneath her. According to McGriff, "At intervals Sam, good businessman that he was, entertained his 'writers' in his fine home. Ruby didn't like that: uncouth niggers getting drunk, messing up her house."[29]

From these contemporary observations, it is apparent that Ruby McCollum was aware that her race was an impediment to her ambition. While she had broken through the glass ceiling that prevented the vast majority of women of her time from being an equal business partner with her husband and succeeding financially, her most desperate attempts could never succeed at breaking through the adamantine ceiling of race in the Jim Crow South.

PART II:
PRESENTIST BIAS

CHAPTER 2:
PRESENTIST BIAS

Presentist bias, also referred to as *presentism,* is the fallacy of looking at the actions and morals of the past through the rearview mirror of the present. Revisiting the past to better understand the present is instructive, but studying history solely for the purpose of condemning specific actions can lead to fallacious reasoning.

Advances in civil rights and personal liberty have been bought with the blood of many generations, so when traveling back in time to an era when most of these liberties did not exist for a minority, it is necessary to examine every event within the appropriate historical framework.

To view the case of Ruby McCollum in its proper perspective, it is instructive to travel even farther back in time, to examine the cases of black women who killed white people, and what they faced in the courts of their day.

The Trial of Celia

Kerry Segrave investigates the first recorded example of a trial afforded to an African American woman who killed her white paramour.[30]

In Missouri in 1855, 70-year-old Robert Newsome bought 14-year-old Celia, a female slave, for his personal pleasure and immediately forced sexual relations on her. Over several years, Celia bore two children for Newsome and had just become pregnant with his third child. One night during her pregnancy, she became very ill, and Newsome visited to force sexual relations upon her, ignoring her protests of being too sick to have intercourse. During their struggle, Celia grabbed a fire log and stuck Newsome, killing him instantly.

When the case came to trial, the court was concerned only about a single point of law—whether Celia, as legally owned property, had a right to defend herself against her master's assault. After reviewing the facts of the killing, and existing law regarding the rights of owners with regard to their slaves, the trial judge ruled that Celia had no rights over her own body. Because she was Newsome's property, she should have submitted to her master's demands regardless of any pain that this might have caused her.

The trial ended with Celia being convicted of murder and executed by hanging on December 21, 1855.

While this trial is incomprehensible by today's standards, it must nonetheless be considered a fair and just trial in that it conformed to the law of the time. As many slave owners pointed out, the ruling was also supported by the writings of Paul in his epistles (both Ephesians 6:5 and Colossians 3:22), where he admonishes slaves to obey their masters.

The Trial of Ann Boston

Segrave reports on the various versions reported in the press when Ann Boston (also known as Anne Bostwick), an African American woman living after the Civil War, stabbed to death Mrs. R. R. Jordan, the wife of a prominent planter, on the afternoon of June 25, 1912, in Pinehurst, Georgia.[31] The first newspaper coverage of the story was in Macon, Georgia, in an article that commented on Bostwick's sanity:

> While living here [Fort Valley] the lynched Negress was tried by a jury and found a fit subject for the lunatic asylum but owning to the crowded condition of that institution she could not be received. In her rational moments she was a good reliable servant, but became violent at times.[32]

Several other newspapers reported that the lynch mob was led by women driving expensive automobiles and that Celia was executed by a group of men who assisted them. No charges were filed.

This led Henry Watterson, editor of the *Louisville Courier-Journal,* to state that "the ends of justice were served," but he added that he felt that peace would have been better conserved in Georgia by the prosecution of the woman and the legal hanging that would "certainly" have resulted. Watterson concluded, "But the method was that of savages and savagery begets reprisal in kind. There is always greater probability of lawlessness where lawless methods are employed by the determined citizens."[33]

While Watterson, representing the white press, commented on Bostwick's sanity and the denial of a trial, he did not question her ultimate punishment of death by hanging—it was the means, not the ends, that he questioned.

A far different version of the story was reported by Mae Clide, an African American reporter for the *Chicago Defender*, a black newspaper in its infancy at the time.[34] According to Clide, Mrs. Jordan, Boston's employer, was in the habit of slapping her face and otherwise abusing her and had injured her severely on several occasions: "The servant at last, goaded beyond endurance with pain and anger, took the life of her employer by stabbing her."

Clide was the first to report abuse as the cause of Bostwick's attack on her employer, rather than Bostwick's supposed insanity, which the white press blamed for the murder.

In the same article, Clide also observed that black servants were hired in the area for as little as fifty cents a week and never over four dollars a month. At these salaries, they were required to do all the housework, washing, ironing, and chores; attend the children; "and suffer any humiliation that the educated(?) and charitable(?) white women are pleased to thrust upon her. Her position in the house of such Christian(?) people can better be imagined than described."

Clide continues, "In truth, when one enters the home of a southern white as a servant it is as Dante says in his *Inferno*, namely 'All hope is lost, ye who enter here.'" Clide supports this characterization by listing a host of humiliations faced by blacks in the South, including a litany of Jim Crow laws preventing them from exercising most of the civil rights that whites took for granted.

Clide concludes, "And every lick they get from us is not amiss."

Ann Boston's is the first case of an African American woman killing a white person in which the African American press, like the *Pittsburgh Courier* many years later, could investigate the story and debunk the white version of an interracial murder with a "Negress" as the suspect.

The Trial of Ruby McCollum

An example of a presentist take on Ruby McCollum's trial occurs in the docudrama, *The Shot Doctor,* when Tammy Evans comments on the trial: "The judge said, 'This trial will be done fair and square and in accordance with the law.' Well, it appears that it depends on the definition of fairness and whose law."[35]

This retrospective approach to history fails to consider that 1950s standards of jurisprudence, while far more enlightened than a century earlier, were still less considerate of the civil rights of African Americans than years later, in a Miranda right, post-Jim Crow era.

Because of this, Ruby McCollum's trial must be measured by the definition of fairness and the nature of the law in the 1950s, and not by the definition of fairness and the nature of the law in the early twenty-first century.

In the same documentary, Dr. Evans asserts that Ruby McCollum was silenced, by parroting Hurston's rhetoric about how many times McCollum was prevented from answering her attorney's questions. But what Evans *doesn't* mention is that this was the first time since the 13th, 14th, and 15th

Amendments to the Constitution that an African American woman was not only allowed on the stand, but was also allowed to testify to the advances of a white man who abused her and forced her to have his child.

Finally, Evans overlooks the fact that this was the first trial in the history of Suwannee County in which African Americans were summoned as jurors. All eight of the black veniremen, however, objected to the death penalty in order to be dismissed from serving on the jury. This first attempt at a trial was aborted when Ruby McCollum's attorney, Pigeye Crews, was temporarily disbarred.[36]

During the second attempt at a trial, seven of the African American veniremen called to court were disqualified based on their statements that that they had been patients of Dr. LeRoy Adams, while the eighth was qualified as an alternate juror.[37] When Crews objected that his client could not be tried by a jury of her peers and that there should be a change of venue, Judge Adams had this to say:

> On this point it is the long and well established law in Florida that a Defendant is not entitled to any certain juror to try him from any certain class or race of people. If it were not that way, a Defendant who happened to be of another race of people other than our people—like a Frenchman, Italian or a Russian—if there were no Frenchmen, Italians or Russians in said county where he was to be tried, he would have the right to have his case transferred to some other county where they might have some members of his race. In this matter we had quite a number of Colored men who were served with process and appeared and were examined. They were all disqualified upon their own statements as to their association with Dr. Adams; all of them stating that he was their regular family physician; that they called him in many instances and at all times in case of sickness in their home. The Court knew those Colored men and knew they were pretty substantial men among their race of people. One or two of them are leaders among their people and they are looked upon as good, solid men. White people look upon them as being good, solid men. They disqualified themselves, all except this Colored man, Box, I believe. He had not used the Doctor. He apparently qualified just as fully as the balance of them did. His name is on the list somewhere. I don't know where it is or what part of the list it is on, but he is subject to call according to the list. I know of no requirement of law that I should put this juror's name or order the Clerk to put this juror's name in a different place than it naturally appears on this list as it was drawn. However, there has been no discrimination. There has been no partiality; there has been no attempt to keep this juror out of the box. He would come in it in due course if we get down to his name on the list, but we haven't got down there yet. If we do, he will go into the box and through the same process as any other juror, just exactly, and with no exceptions.[38]

In spite of these statements, it is clear that the elephant in the room was race. An electronic search of the text of the trial transcript reveals that the word "race" appears 20 times, "white" appears 158 times, "Negro" appears 10 times, and "colored" appears 227 times, reflecting the court's awareness of the importance of race in this nationally publicized case.

In spite of this underlying racial tone, Ruby McCollum's trial remains the first murder trial in the segregationist South in which a woman of color was allowed to take the stand and bear witness against a white man who forced her to have his children.

Although these aspects of the trial are not acknowledged by Evans or others, if viewed in the proper context of justice in the Jim Crow South, they were groundbreaking. Moreover, placed within the context of its time and place, the trial was hardly the epitome of unfairness and the violation of trial law that her words imply by invoking present-day standards.

In fact, this trial is an excellent example of the way that social change happens—one painful, halting step at a time.

From Celia to Ann, to Ruby—from being considered a white man's property to being lynched without a trial, to having a trial and being able to testify that she killed in self-defense—there is evidence of the slow march of social justice toward equality in a future that has not yet arrived.

Presentist Bias and Domestic Abuse

Another example of presentist bias occurs in portraying McCollum's abuse by Adams outside its historical context.

Domestic abuse was widespread in the 1950s, a time when basically no laws against it were on the books. A man could beat his wife into submission, as many did, and the woman had no recourse in the law.

Ruby McCollum related to her African American attorney, Releford McGriff, that her husband "took her down a peg" from time to time and would demean her in front of his men.[39]

It is through the prevailing attitudes toward domestic violence *at that time,* not today's attitudes, that we must analyze McCollum's abuse, yet many who weigh in on the subject choose to ignore Sam McCollum's abuse of his wife in their narrative, while emphasizing the abuse she received from Adams.

Presentist Bias and Ruby McCollum's Psychological Condition

Ruby's psychological condition will be discussed in this section on presentist bias and again in chapter 3, from the standpoint of confirmation bias.

A newspaper article reviewing the documentary, *You Belong to Me,* asks, "Was Wealthy Black Woman Driven Crazy to Shoot White Doctor in Head in 1952?"[40] Aside from the sloppy journalism involved in asserting that Adams was shot in the head when he was actually shot in the back, the article states that Adams had a "friend" deliver McCollum's baby by him when, in fact, it was Adams's cousin, a physician who owned a hospital in Valdosta, Georgia.[41]

According to available records, the first mention of any psychological problem suffered by Ruby McCollum was in her trial, when her attorney, P. Guy Crews, sought Judge Adams's permission to ask Dr. McCullagh, a Jacksonville psychiatrist, to join the court-appointed physicians tasked with evaluating Ruby McCollum's mental state. Crews cited the following to Judge Adams:

> I have been informed that Dr. McCullagh of Jacksonville, who is a recognized psychiatrist in the treatment of mental diseases, has a case history on this Defendant, which was made about a month prior to this occurrence and while she was confined in Brewster Hospital in Jacksonville, to the effect that she exhibited a desire for a specific nurse and when she was denied that nurse she left the hospital under an hallucination—I will say it is an hallucination—because she left under the apprehension or misapprehension that the nurses other than the one she preferred were trying to poison her.[42]

Judge Adams agreed that Dr. McCullagh could join the team of psychiatrists to examine McCollum since he had treated her several times earlier in the year when Adams had admitted her to the psychiatric ward of the Negro Brewster Hospital in Jacksonville.

This is the first mention of Ruby McCollum believing that she was being poisoned, although she would later, in her letters written from the Suwannee Jail, accuse Dr. Adams, as well as the personnel at Brewster Hospital, Raiford, and the Suwannee County Jail, of poisoning her.

Chapter 3 details the list of medications that she alleged Adams gave her, as well as those that she alleged were given her while she was institutionalized, and the pharmacological effects of each medication that can be verified.

When the psychiatrists reported to the court, Judge Adams read their summaries and determined that McCollum was "sane and in full possession of her mental faculties."[43]

On October 6, 1952, when Crews called Dr. McCullagh to testify during the sanity hearing, McCullagh testified regarding McCollum's multiple admissions to Jacksonville's Brewster Hospital for coloreds before the murder:

> A. She was there first in January where she was a patient for about 12 days I think, and again in February where she was there about 9 days, and I think she was there on a third occasion in May when she was there about a week. That was all in 1952.
>
> Q. That was January, February and May of this year?
>
> A. Yes, Sir.
>
> Q. And what did you find to be wrong with her?
>
> A. I can tell you what I meant by depression and hypochondria. By depression I meant she was emotionally despondent or blue and worrying, and by hypochondria I mean that she was preoccupied with feelings that she was having. For example, she was complaining of discomfort of her chest, but X-rays of her chest and examination of her heart and lungs and blood pressure was made and nothing was found. She was also complaining of pain in her back and lower abdomen and we made studies of that area and many X-rays of that area which were interpreted to be normal.
>
> Q. And that is what you meant by psychoneurosis and hypochondria?
>
> A. Yes, Sir.[44]

McCullagh's diagnosis of hypochondria resulted from his determination that no physical causes could be found for her various aches and pains.

The psychological nomenclature that Dr. McCullagh uses in this testimony is based on the psychoanalytic model of psychiatry practiced when the first *Diagnostic and Statistical Manual* (DSM-I) was introduced by the American Psychiatric Association in 1952.

At that time, in the DSM-1, "psychoneurosis" included the following disorders:

- psychoneurotic reactions
- anxiety reaction
- dissociative reaction
- conversion reaction
- phobic reaction
- obsessive-compulsive reaction
- depressive reaction
- psychoneurotic reaction

While these disorders were poorly defined and not grouped according to today's DSM-V (soon to be DSM-VI) standards, one of the above-listed disorders—conversion reaction—is a state in which a person's psychological stress manifests in physical symptoms. Symptoms of the other disorders listed include anxiety, depression, and phobia, all of which McCollum exhibited when she thought that people were trying to poison her in the hospital.

By any standard, it is clear that Ruby McCollum was under severe stress, although she did not appear to be forthcoming in stating the nature of the stresses that she was facing—other than the fact that she thought she was being poisoned both by Adams and by employees of all the institutions where she was housed.

McCollum's stay in the mental ward at Brewster Hospital could not, under any circumstances, be described as a "rest," as Evans puts it.[45] When William Huie spoke to an unnamed nurse at Brewster Hospital who had cared for McCollum, she told him:

— Yes, I nursed poor Ruby several times [the nurse told me]. I know all about her. I listened to her talk by the hour, both when she was clear and when she was delirious. Dr. Adams had her on some sort of dope, and she carried it in a little bag tied around her neck. With all mental patients, we are supposed to take *everything* away from them when they enter the hospital. But we just couldn't get this medicine away from Ruby. She'd fight us; and we'd try to sneak up on her when she was asleep and get it. No matter how sound asleep she appeared to be, when we started to try to get that thing from around her neck, she'd wake right up and resist us.

— She'd stay in the hospital only as long as that medicine lasted. Then she'd get out, and go back to Live Oak, and get another supply from Dr. Adams.

— She'd talk for hours about her children, and her home, and about what a good husband she had, though she said her husband was gone a lot. She carried pictures of this little white child with her all the time, kept 'em under her pillow, and she'd insist that we look at 'em almost every day . . .

— When she come back in May, she was in bad shape, getting worse all the time. She talked about Dr. Adams and how he was gonna be governor. But she didn't really start cracking up until June, when she learned she was pregnant again. She had menstruated while she was at the hospital in May, but she didn't in June, and it worried her. She didn't want any more children—but she said that she just couldn't help it—that the doctor was the "boss." She couldn't see nothing but more pain and trouble ahead of her, and we couldn't cheer her up.

— We were giving her insulin shock treatments so heavy that we kept a pitcher of orange juice at the bedside to bring her back in case she sank too deep. She was one troubled soul.[46]

While it is impossible to diagnose Ruby McCollum's condition, her symptoms are quite similar to those of someone undergoing what is today known as an "adult situational crisis," more commonly known as a "mental breakdown."

From many standpoints, it is understandable that Ruby McCollum was under increasing stress during early 1952:

1. McCollum had a husband who cheated on her and had distanced himself from her in an "arrangement" to let her continue her own affair after she had a "white" baby by Adams.[47]

2. In Adams, she had a lover who supplied her with drugs but who was also becoming increasingly abusive and then distancing himself from her while taking increasing amounts of her money to mount his senatorial campaign.

3. The Federal Revenue Act, enacted in October 1951, forced Sam McCollum to register with the federal government as an operator of a gambling operation, buy a federal license or "tax stamps," and submit to periodic audits of his books and pay the IRS a 10 percent tax on their gross operation.[48] This meant that operators had to pay the tax not only on their profits but also on the moneys that they paid out to winners.

4. Certainly, business would fall off drastically if Sam continued to record the names of law enforcement people who received money as payoffs. The alternative was not to report the names of law enforcement personnel receiving payouts, pay them under the table and off the books, and then pay taxes on those cash payouts as if he had kept the cash as profit. The same would apply to payouts to winners and writers of the bolita tickets who would not want their names revealed.

The numbers tell the story.

According to Huie, the McCollums kept one-fourth of the gross, paid out one-fourth for winnings, paid one-fourth to the writers of the bolita tickets, and paid one-fourth to law enforcement.[49] Now, under the new federal law, the McCollums were suddenly responsible for a 10 percent tax on the gross with no deductions. This resulted in a 40 percent reduction in their usual profit, and this did not even account for the money that Adams was taking for his campaign, the McCollums' generous donations to their church, or the "no-interest loans" they extended to the white business community.

This fact must have been painfully obvious to Ruby McCollum as the keeper of the books.

On top of all of this, the Associated Press carried the names of 322 Florida residents who had bought the federally mandated gambling stamps, and the *Suwannee Democrat* ran this front-page headline on January 11, 1952: "Ten Live Oak Negroes Procure Gambling Stamps: 'Bolita Sam' and Crew Sign Up."[50] In the same article, Louie Wadsworth, owner of the newspaper and longtime crusader against bolita, announced, "The federal government has flushed out those engaged in gambling into the open. State law prohibits gambling other than at race tracks."

The article continued to implicate local whites and law enforcement in bolita, maintaining that gambling could not be operated by the newly registered colored operators without assistance from the white community, and asking the citizens of Live Oak to point fingers at those involved.

This sort of financial loss and public embarrassment at being not only outed but also identified as having illegal business dealings in both the state and the county must have been devastating for Ruby McCollum.

In early 1952, Adams had his own problems when his son, Clifford LeRoy Adams III ("Sonny"), was in an automobile accident on January 31 and died the next day.[51] According to Huie, Edith Park, Adams's nurse, maintained that Adams used his son's death to gain sympathy during his campaign.[52]

Park also reported:

> I honestly think Dr. Adams was trying to become a better citizen. I noticed great changes in 1952. The death of his son seemed to soften him. It seemed like he was growing kinder to Florrie Lee. He took Florrie Lee out on calls now—instead of Evelyn. The day after the boy's funeral people came to his house to sympathize. He seemed to feel some affection for her. She said to a friend, "If only LeRoy and I could have been closer, maybe this wouldn't have happened."[53]

This left little room for Ruby McCollum. But she was not to be put off so easily as Adams's white girlfriend, whose silence was bought with a car, a house for her mother, and a job running his boarding house in Lake City.

According to Thelma Curry, Adams's black office assistant, McCollum began visiting the office daily.[54] Clearly, Ruby McCollum had become a problem for Adams—and as a physician he had the means to get her out of town.

According to the testimony of the psychiatrist Dr. McCullagh, Adams first admitted McCollum to the mental ward at Brewster, a Jacksonville hospital for coloreds, in January for about 12 days, in February for about 9 days, and in May for about 7 days.[55]

McCollum's first admission coincided with when her husband was forced to register his business with the feds and be outed in a state and a county where his operations were illegal. The final blow came after her last admission, when, according to the same nurse at Brewster who spoke with Huie, she found out in June that she was pregnant with her second child by Adams.[56]

Ruby's pregnancy proves that she and Adams had at least one sexual encounter in May after she was discharged from Brewster. When she told her husband that she was pregnant again by Adams, he threatened to kill her if she had another baby by him. When she told Adams and asked for an abortion, he denied her an abortion and threatened to kill her if she sought one elsewhere. She was, in her own words, "caught between two guns."[57]

Then, in July, Adams flew to the Democratic National Convention, leaving her alone to worry about her dwindling finances, the publicly announced illegality of the McCollum business, and her pregnancy with a second child by him, with no supply of drugs to numb her pain.[58]

In the weeks leading up to the fateful day, there was a widely held belief in the town that either Ruby McCollum was going to shoot Adams, or Adams was going to shoot her:

1. LaVergne Blue told Huie, "I knew that Ruby's last child had been his, and I knew that a situation was building up where a man could get shot."[59]

2. On this topic, Huie also mentions that an informant stated that Adams bragged of his baby by Ruby and said that he had gotten her pregnant again.

    > He also said that Ruby McCollum was very jealous of him, and that she was
    > jealous of the white girl that Dr. Adams was keeping in Lake City, Florida,
    > and I told him that she was likely to kill him and he replied, 'No such stuff
    > as that,' and about two weeks after this conversation, I got a telephone call
    > that Ruby McCollum had killed Dr. Adams.

3. After her investigation of the murder in Live Oak, Hurston later wrote Huie, predicting that he would find that "he [Adams] and Black plot Ruby's murder out at Adams's farm."[60]

4. Edith Park, Adams's nurse, told Huie that Adams was planning to kill McCollum.[61]

5. Houston Roberts, one of the owners of a local hardware store, told Huie that Adams was pressing him to order a .410 pistol when he came back from the Democratic National Convention in July, even though he already had a handgun, which he carried in the glove compartment of his car. But the .410 pistol fired a small-bore shotgun round, which could not be traced by ballistics.[62]

During the last days of July through the first days of August, right after Adams returned from the Democratic National Convention, tensions between Adams and McCollum escalated:

1. On Wednesday or Thursday of that week, Thelma Curry, an office assistant, heard McCollum demand an abortion from Adams. In response, he hit her so hard, she fell to the floor.[63]

2. During the week of the murder, Adams pressured Houston Roberts for the .410 pistol that he had ordered.

3. On Saturday morning before the murder, McCollum received a bill from Adams's office, addressed to her husband. According to Huie's source, Adams scrawled a note at the bottom of the bill telling Sam to keep her out of his office, and calling her, "crazy as a bat."[64]

4. What Huie was not told was that the bill also had a charge for a D and C—a charge of one hundred sixteen dollars, which far exceeded a month of office visits at three dollars per visit—which McCollum wanted desperately to know about, since she suspected that her husband had agreed to pay for his girlfriend's abortion, though she had no proof.[65] This accounts for her testimony, during her trial, that she paid Adams nine dollars for her three office visits, then asked about the bill to her husband for one hundred sixteen dollars. During the trial, she testified that she asked, "May I peep and see who made that bill?"[66] This clearly indicates that she knew that her husband was not the patient, and only by seeing the patient ledger could she confirm her suspicions that his he had paid for a D&C—i.e., abortion—for his girlfriend.

5. That same Saturday morning, McCollum banged on the operating-room door at the Suwannee County Hospital, demanding to see Adams. Adams yelled to a nurse, "Tell that

goddamn nigger woman to go to hell!" Then, after ordering the nurse to close up the patient, he hurried down the hall in a fury and punched Dr. Sims, a fellow physician who had approached him about an unrelated problem.[67]

6. McCollum then stayed up all Saturday night, trying to telephone Adams. One operator reported placing forty calls for McCollum.[68] After over a hundred frantic calls over the course of several hours, the switchboard operators refused to place any more calls for her.[69]

Ruby McCollum's world was crumbling around her, and there was nothing she could do to regain control.

PART III:

CONFIRMATION BIAS

CHAPTER 3:
INSTANCES OF CONFIRMATION BIAS

Confirmation bias results when a researcher starts the investigation with a desired conclusion in mind, then looks for and reports only the data supporting that conclusion.

Confirmation bias is the view of the beholder standing before J. K. Rowling's mirror of Erised and seeing only what his or her heart most deeply desires.

Perhaps the most egregious example of confirmation bias concerning the Ruby McCollum case occurs in "The Shot Doctor," a 2014 episode in the *Crime to Remember* series on the Discovery ID channel. In this episode, in which I appeared, the narrator comments on the prosecution's objections to McCollum's testimony during her trial: "This silencing of Ruby, keeping her from telling her side of the story, has led to speculation that there was something even more duplicitous going on—like maybe Ruby didn't shoot Doc Adams at all."[3]

I had informed the producers in advance that Ruby McCollum had testified at her trial, and that she was allowed to speak about her affair with Adams, his abuse of her, and his forcing her to bear his children. I also told them that she had refused to speak to a Jacksonville newspaper reporter who visited her during her stay at the state penitentiary in Raiford prior to her trial. But all of this hit the proverbial editing-room floor in favor of a tightly scripted rewrite of history. For the Ruby McCollum story is much more dramatic, more poignant, if it can rise to the level of *To Kill a Mockingbird,* in which the African American on trial is an innocent victim, and the entire community has risen up to protect the perpetrator of a monstrous crime.

Confirmation Bias and "Speaking out of Turn"

In her dissertation turn book, *The Silencing of Ruby McCollum: Race, Class, and Gender in the South,* Dr. Tammy Evans writes about the hard lessons that people, black or white, who spoke out of turn learned in the racially tense Jim Crow South:

> McCollum tried to do it, and she was committed to a mental institution. Huie
> tried to do it, and he was jailed for contempt of court. Zora Neale Hurston,

then a reporter for the *Pittsburgh Courier,* tried to do it, and she fled the community in fear for her life. The national media tried to do it, and citizens closed their ranks with the unanimous refrain 'no comment.'[70]

Unfortunately, regardless of the rhetorical construct of her statements, none of them are based on the facts:

1. McCollum was not committed to Chattahoochee for speaking out of turn. She was committed because her mental deterioration while she was incarcerated had progressed to the point that she was nonresponsive, could not manage her own hygiene, would not eat, and lashed out and struck the examining psychiatrist before her second trial, leading to the determination that she was incapable of participating in her own defense.[71]

2. Huie was not found in contempt of court for simply "speaking out of turn," nor was he jailed on a contempt charge. Huie's problem began when he was found in contempt of court for speaking privately with Dr. Fernay, the psychiatrist who had examined Ruby for the court, and maintaining that there were illegal dealings between Judge Adams and Dr. Adams. The judge was furious after Fernay spoke with him, and issued a contempt charge against Huie for witness tampering. When Huie appeared before the court for the contempt charge on October 9, 1954, he refused to pay the fine, demanding instead to spend time in jail. The judge knew Huie's reputation well enough to know that this was a publicity stunt and told him to get out of the courtroom and come back when he was ready to pay the fine. Huie then stormed out of the courtroom and walked directly across the street to the Western Auto store, where he bought a roll of duct tape. He then went to his car and taped the horn ring down to the steering wheel. On his third trip around the courthouse with his horn blaring, Sheriff Sim Howell arrested Huie—not for contempt of court—but for disturbing the peace. This ended Huie's version of the Battle of Jericho that made him the talk of the town and gave him the jail time he wanted. By his own account, the decision to defy the court and not pay the fine resulted in his incarceration--but he left out the rest of the story, allowing his publicist to say that he was jailed on a contempt charge and, decades later, for Evans to fall for the publicity stunt and write that he was silenced since he "spoke out of turn."[72]

3. Hurston did not flea Live Oak out of fear for her life for "speaking out of turn." She left Live Oak only after the trial and only when she failed to receive money owed her by the *Pittsburgh Courier*. In a letter to Huie, dated March 28, 1954, Hurston writes:

> When the *Pittsburgh Courier* both wired and wrote me urging me to report the case for them, I told them my fee would be $1,000. They put up a poor mouth, but finally agreed to pay it in installments. In the end and after many agonizing delays, I have received in small sums, a little over $200. I lost out on both my land and my car. As Mr. Cannon could tell you, they even left me stranded in hostile Live Oak for two days before the money was sent to enable me to get back to Eau Gallie.[73]

Even though Hurston describes Live Oak as "hostile," she does not write that she "fled the community in fear for her life," as Evans contends.

Also, in the remaining fragment of a letter dated May 28, 1953, to William Nunn, the editor of the *Courier,* Hurston lambastes him for attributing statements to her that she did not make, and confronts him by stating that she was "not even decently paid for what I did."[74] In fact, she later wrote to Huie, telling him that she did not have bus fare to travel to Live Oak to attend the second trial.[75] She also wrote in a letter to Huie, dated May, 14, 1954, "I was, and am not afraid to appear in Live Oak, but wondered if you really wanted me there, or just was being nice and polite."[76] Then, in a letter to Huie dated July 1, 1954, Hurston writes, "I will be there at the trial."[77]

It is apparent that even though Hurston considered Live Oak "hostile," she wanted to travel there for the second trial and was not afraid to do so. Unfortunately, she could not afford the bus fare, and Huie did not offer to help.

Also, Evans and others have evidently ignored what Huie wrote about Judge Adams fearing for his own life:

> The case has been a tribulation for me. My life was threatened. I received insolent letters from Negroes in Chicago and Philadelphia, making vile remarks to me, and threatening to kill me. It isn't pleasant to have your life threatened. It worried my wife.[78]

4. The citizens of Live Oak did not close ranks with a "unanimous refrain of 'no comment.'" In an article appearing in the September 20, 1952, issue of the *Pittsburgh Courier,* reporters Clay and Rivera wrote of their experience in Live Oak:

> From one end of Live Oak to another, wherever we talked to people no matter who they were, they told us they thought the Sabbath morning tragedy was the result of a romance Mrs. McCollum had become involved in with the doctor.
>
> We heard also that it was an open secret that Sam McCollum had not been "getting along with his wife lately."[79]

A reporter from the *New York Post* also spoke to members of the community in Live Oak and published his account of the murder.[80] So it's obvious that many citizens of Live Oak spoke freely with members of the press.

It is unfortunate that because of her confirmation bias, Evans chose to craft a dramatic yet erroneous statement that Ruby McCollum was silenced and others were punished for "speaking out of turn" as the groundwork for her dissertation turned book, rather than rely on the facts.

Ruby McCollum did more than "speak out of turn" to land herself in hot water. In choosing a white paramour, Ruby McCollum crossed cultural boundaries. More importantly, she made the unfortunate and unknowing choice of a politically powerful sociopath as her "big man," and this choice, not "speaking out of turn," was her ultimate undoing.

Confirmation Bias and the Question of Rape

Many recent feminist accounts of Ruby McCollum's story paint a picture of an abused African American woman who was trapped in an affair not of her own making and who was repeatedly raped for years.

In the documentary *You Belong to Me: Sex, Race and Murder in the South,* for example, the confirmation bias of the producer, Jude Hagin, is apparent when she interviews McCollum's son, Sam Jr., regarding his mother's choice to have an affair with Adams. As a researcher, her question should have been, "Do you think your mother chose to have an affair with Dr. Adams, or do you think he raped her?" Instead, she began with what she characterized as "my truth": "I'll never believe that your mother had a relationship, willingly, with Dr. Adams. I believe he forced her. That's just how I feel about it."[81]

Despite this leading statement containing Hagin's desired conclusion, Sam Jr. practically laughs at the notion of rape: "Well, [stifled laughter] I guess if you really know anything about men and women's relationship . . . ah . . . being a doctor, I'm sure that he could have tempted her in some way or another, even on examination. This is why nowadays doctors don't examine females by themselves; they always have to have assistants."[82]

Sam McCollum Jr.'s assessment recalls Henry Kissinger's axiom that power is the ultimate aphrodisiac. Certainly, a powerful white man was the ultimate aphrodisiac for Ruby McCollum, who, in her own words, picked her men "from the top."[83]

Hagin responds to McCollum's assessment of the affair in a voiceover: "Sam had shed his truth with me and something else had happened, something I had not realized was so important: I had shared my truth with him."

It is apparent that Hagin is not looking for archival history in her documentary. She is looking to confirm a very personally held "truth." In other words, she is approaching the story with an unshakable confirmation bias.

And Hagin is not alone in reaching her own personal "truth" regardless of the facts. Ruth Thompson-Miller, an associate professor at the University of Ohio in Dayton, makes the following impassioned statement in the documentary *You Belong to Me*:

> Ruby McCollum was raped. When you have a history of the raping of black women in this country in the South the way it was for Ruby McCollum, I don't care what anybody says. Living with the fear of not doing what a white man told you to do was death—not just death for you, but death for your family, burn your house down, hurt your kids.[84]

Based on the foregoing assumption, in chapter 2 of a classroom study guide written as a companion for the documentary, she then asks her students, "In the documentary, give examples of where you think Ruby had the power to say no."[85]

After hearing their professor state passionately, "Ruby McCollum was raped," followed by "I don't care what anybody says," what student would dare differ with an authority figure who issues their grade for the course?

And what academician leading young, formative minds to develop the skill of critical thinking asserts, "I don't care what anybody says," and then expects an intelligent discourse to ensue? It is apparent that any attempt to approach the question logically has been peremptorily dismissed.

What Thompson-Miller fails to present to her students is that Ruby McCollum was no ordinary colored woman and that there is absolutely no evidence that she was raped.

By her assertion "I don't care what anybody says," Thompson-Miller totally ignores the following accounts of Ruby McCollum's affair with Adams:

1. Releford McGriff, the McCollum family friend, business associate, and African American attorney, speaks of the affair:

> Ruby's ego needed nourishment. Adams was a big shot, headed for the governor's chair. When he extended an "examination" in her upstairs bedroom—I don't want to malign a client, but I doubt that Ruby's resistance was more than token.
>
> Even today, wasting away up there in that jail, half crazy; sometimes when she's talking to me Ruby's eyes will flash and she will say, "I pick my men off the top! Black or white, I get the Big Men!"[86]

Also, during the wrongful-death lawsuit brought by Adams's widow against the McCollum estate, McGriff relates that Ms. Adams, a rather strait-laced Southern lady as I remember her from church, was asked if her husband was "vigorous," since, in the eyes of the law at the time, a vigorous man was worth more than one who was not. McGriff recounts that moment in the trial when Ms. Adams struggled through her embarrassment to respond to the question:

> I heard Ruby say, under her breath, 'No doubt about that.' I almost popped. I had to put my head in my arms to keep the judge from seeing me laughing and fining me for contempt.[87]

Even though not on the stand, Ruby McCollum was evidently more qualified to testify to Adams's sexual prowess than his wife. These are not the words of a woman who was continually subjected to the trauma of rape for over five years.

McGriff summarized the ultimate tragedy of Ruby's affair with Adams:

> Ruby's tragedy comes from her being a little too well educated, a little too proud for her own good. What's happened to her has happened to other Negro women—and other white women—but heretofore the Negro women have been simple enough, and uneducated, and helpless, so they have had to take it. Ruby couldn't take it.[88]

McGriff established that Ruby McCollum is not to be placed among the "simple enough, and uneducated, and helpless" Negro women of her time, as so many of today's academics, writers, and documentary producers contend.

McGriff goes on to describe Ruby as intellectually superior to Sam. And when Sam started fooling around with younger, lighter-skinned women:

> …that was Ruby's first cross to bear…. I guess most thirty-five-year-old housewives find it unpleasant to be sexually neglected. But to be rich, arrogant, and also neglected is just about unbearable for a Ruby. Moreover, Sam, on occasion, 'took her down a peg.'[89]

2. Sam McCollum's African American schoolteacher girlfriend, Lucy Brown, was certainly in a position to know him better than anyone but his wife. When Huie interviewed her, she spoke of when Sam McCollum discovered that his wife had a baby by Adams:

> Sam was stunned when Ruby's fourth child 'came white.' He just couldn't believe it. He came here the next night, and he was badly shaken. He kept moaning that he just couldn't believe that Ruby would do it to him.[90]

Brown further describes his dilemma:

> When the baby was born and Sam found out what Ruby was doing, what could he do? He could kill Adams and lose everything, including his life. He could kill Ruby or drive her out, but he loved her and he loved his home. So he had a sorry choice: for business and other reasons, he just had to take it. He had to work out an "arrangement" with Ruby for carrying on.[91]

From the account of a woman who was intimate with Sam McCollum for years, Sam was unaware of the affair between his wife and Adams until Loretta was born.

Sam McCollum's girlfriend was also quite clear about her take on the McCollums as a couple:

> That was Ruby's and Sam's tragedy. They both had to have outside sexual interests to support their pride, and that won't work. Maybe it ought to work—but it won't—and a woman

as smart as Ruby ought to know it. Maybe what's good for the gander ought to be good for the goose, but it isn't. Sam wanted to keep his wife and his home and his children and also have his "girl." Maybe that's wrong. Maybe it's arrogant on a man's part. But it's the way some men are; and women ought to recognize it.[92]

Regarding who was to blame, she pointed to Ruby McCollum's ambition:

> Ruby wanted *everything*. Well, maybe she can get everything in Heaven. But on earth human beings just have to do the best we can . . .
> Ruby fell down on her part. I'm sorry for her. But she made her bed. She hurt Sam and fouled up her home.[93]

First, Sam McCollum's girlfriend clearly blames Ruby for the affair with Adams. At no point does she indicate that Sam ever told her it was rape. Second, the reference is clear that from the start of the affair to Loretta's birth, Sam McCollum had no idea that his wife and Adams were having an affair. This was about two years before the murder.

3. Lucy Brown's account of the McCollum-Adams affair clearly coincides with the timeline that *Pittsburgh Courier* reporter Revella Clay reports in an interview with "close friends" of Sam McCollum. In her article "Insanity Plea Filed for Ruby," appearing in the September 27, 1952, issue, Clay reports that she was told, "For the last two years, they hadn't been getting along."[94]

    After Loretta was born, Ruby's appearance took a nosedive. Her arrangement with her husband marked the beginning of the marriage's rapid deterioration. And, according to Lucy Brown, "When Adams began beating her up, making her bear his children, and pushing her aside, she couldn't take it. It made her look like a fool; it hurt her pride, and that she couldn't take."[95]

4. During her stay in Live Oak, Zora Hurston spoke with many people, many of whom asked to not be quoted, since they had to live in the community. From her conversations with locals, she expressed her insight into the roles of McCollum and Adams in their tragic story in a letter to Huie dated May 14, 1954: "I suspect that two ruthless individuals met and tangled in Ruby and Dr. Adams. Perhaps egotistical is a better word, or does it add up to the same thing?"[96]

In a letter to Huie dated June 10, 1954, Hurston also speaks directly to Ruby McCollum's role in the affair: "Though abhorring what she did, I was and am sorry for the poor thing. She was a woman terribly in love, and with us females, that makes strange and terrible creatures of us."[97]

Hurston adds to this sentiment in another letter to Huie, dated July 1, 1954: "The dumbest thing a woman can do is to refuse to fade out of the picture when the man is through with her. Certainly accounts for a lot of murders. I sensed this stubbornness in her by little things."[98]

Hurston also writes to Huie about local talk in a "Negro café," regarding McCollum and Adams. One man rails: "Naw, she had to go and have that white man, and when she knows so well how these white men don't allow us no chance at all with *their* women. Colored women ought to be proud to stick to their own men and leave these white men alone."[99]

The man was obviously offended at Ruby McCollum's pride, and her rejection of men of her own race while choosing a white man.

5. Adams's colored office worker, Thelma Curry, also corroborates Ruby's pursuing Adams, rather than the reverse. During the trial, when cross-examined by Frank Cannon, Ruby McCollum's attorney, Curry testified:

> Q.   Do you know how many times this Defendant called on Dr. Adams during the three and a half years that you said you had known her?
> A.   The exact number of calls?
> Q.   Yes.
> A.   I don't know the exact number of calls.
> Q.   About how many?
> A.   That is hard to say because she came to the office quite often.
> Q.   During the entire three and a half years?
> A.   Maybe not during the whole time, but some part of the time.
> Q.   What do you mean by quite often?
> A.   Daily.
> Q.   Daily?
> A.   Daily.[100]

Seeking her abuser out daily is not the behavior of a woman who is being continually raped. Instead, she would seek to avoid him.

6. William Huie's recorded 1982 interview with newspaper reporter Brad Rogers—crafted after spending months on the case, interviewing hundreds of people, and writing his book on the story—is also revealing:

    > Ruby had a good education. She was ambitious. Much of what happened to her she brought upon herself. In many ways, she's just as guilty as the doctor. Dr. Adams didn't rape Ruby McCollum. Dr. Adams screwed Ruby McCollum the first time in her own bed in her own home. The woman herself is guilty of all sorts of things, including the crime of murder.[101]

7. Ted Poston, of the *New York Post,* interviewed Ruby McCollum's friends and neighbors on August 29, 1954, about the time of the second trial. One of them said this about her motivation in choosing to have an affair with Adams:

    > "I don't condone what Ruby did," this woman said, "but put yourself in her shoes. Sam was running around, not only with the chippies in Tampa, but he even had regular women right here."
    >
    > "Think what that must have done to Ruby's pride—and she was a proud woman. Here she was better educated than Sam, the real brains behind his success, the mother of his children, and he out chasing chippies."
    >
    > "Remember, too, Ruby was only around 33 and not like you see her today. She had a trim figure, was the best-dressed woman in town, black or white, yet Sam was looking elsewhere."
    >
    > "So, with her pride, if Ruby decided to get even, she probably was proud to pick the biggest man in town—black or white."[102]

    This woman's words about Ruby McCollum's decision "to pick the biggest man in town—black or white" echo McCollum's own words, confided to her attorney, Releford McGriff, about choosing Adams.

8. Frank Cannon, a white man and McCollum's primary attorney, had this to say about Ruby McCollum when he talked with her in the Suwannee County Jail as she slipped into her paranoid behavior:

And then, she had some sort of strange attachment to that doctor. Sometimes, when her mind has seemed clear, I have been questioning her and she'd be answering with a good deal of intelligence; and suddenly she'd change her attitude, look at me like she hated me, and say, "That's me and the doctor's business!" Then she wouldn't answer any more questions. I guess he'd charmed her, like a snake does a bird, or some strange goddam thing.

9. The title of the January 31, 1953, *Pittsburgh Courier* article, "'I Loved Dr. Adams. He Was Not My Enemy,'" by Trezz W. Anderson, reflects McCollum's words spoken to her attorneys, Releford McGriff and Frank Cannon, who shared these words with Anderson.[103]

10. Edith Park, the Suwannee County Hospital nurse anesthetist and Dr. Adams's office nurse, had this to say about Ruby McCollum:

    — I did not suspect the affair with Ruby. Not suspecting, I kidded him once about Ruby having a crush on him—to which he did not answer. She hung around the office to see him and looked at him with worship in her eyes. I wasn't patient with Ruby. One afternoon she wanted B-12 and I got the syringe, and she held back and whimpered that she wanted "the doctor to give it to me."
    — "Don't waste my time, Ruby," I said. "You've got to take this shot or get on out the back door." And I pulled up her sleeve and popped that needle in her arm and she left. Neurotic women, white or colored, I cannot stand.[104]

11. The following sworn affidavit by Ed Morgan, given to William Huie, speaks to Ruby McCollum's love for Adams:

    He also said that Ruby McCollum was very jealous of him, and that she was jealous of the white girl that Dr. Adams was keeping in Lake City, Florida, and I told him that she was likely to kill him and he replied 'No such stuff as that,' and about two weeks after this conversation I got a telephone call that Ruby McCollum had killed Dr. Adams.[105]

12. In the documentary *You Belong to Me,* Ruby McCollum's sister, Lillian Shuman, implicates her in the affair with Adams, saying, "If she hadn't let down her family, she would not have been in that serious trouble."[106]

No fewer than twelve contemporaries of Ruby McCollum, including her own sister, come down on the side of her choosing to have the affair with Adams, her infatuation with him, and her continuing to hang around his office and chase after him after he had decided that their affair was over.

Far from being silent, the citizens of Live Oak, as well as journalists, were talking about the affair between Ruby McCollum and Dr. Adams.

It also appears that even while Adams was trying to distance himself from McCollum, he still found something attractive enough about her to continue the affair, even though their relationship grew more and more dysfunctional as it progressed. Supporting this view is the fact that she learned she was pregnant with her second child by Adams in June, only about a month before his murder on August 3.

From her daily visits to his office, it also appears that she found something attractive about Adams; otherwise, she would not have pursued him when he was clearly trying to reject her.

Over fifty years later, however, people with various axes to grind in a generation that never lived this story, would have a different "truth." In their historical rewrite, these scholars and documentary producers willfully ignore all these voices, including the voice of McCollum herself, to create an even greater silencing of Ruby McCollum than they accuse Live Oak's citizens of.

It is important to note that Ruby McCollum's mention of Adams's abusing and raping her is recorded in only two places: in her testimony during her trial, and in her letters to her attorneys. It must also be recalled that Ruby McCollum instructed her attorneys to use the defense that she herself had crafted, which included allegations of almost six years of abuse and rape at his hands. She also insisted that they use her account of Adams's attack on her in his office on the day of the murder:

He told me to get on the table. I told him, "Well, can I wait until another time," and he said, "No." He said, "I want you to get up there now." I said, "Well, maybe I can't get up there today." He said, "Yes, you can get up there today." Then I told him why, and he ran into me and grabbed me and started pounding me and he began hitting on me and beating on me with his fist, and told me that, "I don't ever intend to do anything else he asked me to do," and I told him, "I do whatever I can when I can." And he continued hitting me, and then he turned around and grabbed the gun and stuck it in my stomach and I pulled it away from him and he snatched it back, and I grabbed it again and the gun went off, and it went off again, when he fell, and it went off again, and he makes out of the room and went and stood up in the door that entered into this room where the chairs are. He stood there awhile and gradually he went down to the floor, and he laid there flat out. He laid something like that. Anyway, when I started out by him, he grabbed the gun out of my hand. When he grabbed the gun out of my hand, I asked him to give me that gun, please, and he wouldn't give it back to me right then. After a while, I asked him for it again and I caught his arm that way, and I don't know anything else that happened.[107]

Knowing that none of the witnesses supported her testimony in this attack in the office, Huie writes:

> But in the courtroom, on trial for her life before the White and Colored societies of Suwannee County, Ruby hid the truth. She was as careful as the State was not to mention the contents of that letter. It was more satisfying—even if it put her in the chair—to say that she shot him because, on a Sunday morning, with three patients in the waiting room, he found her so seductive that he tried to force her onto the table.[108]

Also, McCollum asserts that Adams, while beating her because she would not submit to his sexual advances, grabbed her gun—which she succeeded in wresting from him—that it went off by itself, that after three shots he staggered into the colored waiting room, and that as she tried to leave, he reached up to grab the gun again, and that she has no memory of the final shot. She also fails to mention that all the shots hit him in the back.

Regardless of whether McCollum was colored or white, this testimony of a woman who succeeded in wresting a gun from a man a hundred pounds heavier and a foot taller than her and then managed to shoot him in the back while he was fighting with her defies credulity. Also, that a dying man lying face down on the floor after being shot in the back and stumbling into the waiting room could grab at the gun as she tried to move past him on her way out of the office beggars the imagination.

Regardless of the number of objections made by the prosecution and sustained by the judge, contemporary accounts of the Ruby McCollum story ignore all this disingenuous testimony that *was* allowed into evidence. Only by doing this can they make a case for self-defense.

Confirmation Bias and Ruby's Ability to End the Affair

On Ruby McCollum's ability to get away from Adams, Zora Hurston expresses her opinion very clearly in a letter to William Huie, dated July 28, 1954:

> Granting that Adams had jilted her, and that he was on bad terms with her husband, what was to prevent her from taking several thousand dollars and going North until the stink

died down? Or even permanently? I am certain that is the course I would have followed. She could have easily laid her hands on $50,000 took her small children and disappeared from Live Oak and had her second child by Adams in peace and safety and let the whole affair be forgotten.[110]

While Hurston may not have understood that fifty thousand dollars—a sum that would be at least half a million of today's dollars—would have been small change for Ruby McCollum, her words are those of a rational person, whose judgment is not clouded by the love-hate relationship that McCollum had with Adams.

In fact, Sam McCollum had talked with Ruby about leaving the county, as witnessed by a nurse at Brewster Hospital, where Ruby was admitted on several occasions. This unnamed nurse told William Huie:

> — I talked several times with Ruby's husband, Sam, when he'd come there for her. He paid me well. He seemed to be devoted to her, but awful worried.
>
> "Man, why don't you get this woman out of this country?" I asked him. "You got money. Send her up North somewhere; she's got to have a change."
>
> — And he always said that he was trying to get her to go. He said that he had wanted her to go up and see the last Joe Louis fight. But she wouldn't leave Suwannee County.[109]

But Ruby McCollum refused to make the same choice that the former bolita king of Suwannee County, L. J. Hopps, had made only about a decade earlier when threatened by local whites over teaching black students how to write.[110] His efforts as a teacher at the colored Douglass High School were getting noticed in town, leading to accusations that coloreds were becoming more "uppity." Local whites' suspicions seemed confirmed when William James Howard, a young colored boy, wrote notes on a Christmas card to his white female coworker at Van Priest's department store expressing his feelings toward her, and later wrote a letter of apology to the same girl for sending her the card. The following January, the girl's father and his friends mutilated and drowned Willie James in the Suwannee River in front of his father.

Hopps, sensing the unrest in town months before the drowning, convinced his wife to join him in signing over his house to Sam McCollum for the sum of ten dollars, supposedly because he lost a game of poker to McCollum. The deed for this transaction, transferring three lots and "improvements" to Sam McCollum, is on record at the Suwannee County Courthouse and is reproduced in Appendix C.

But Ruby McCollum was not about to give up her house and leave town in fear for her life as L. J. Hopps and his wife, Beatrice, had done a decade earlier. She chose to stand her ground.

Confirmation Bias and the Question of Ruby McCollum's Being Colonized

Evans states that Adams's "conquest of Ruby was an act of 'colonization,'" citing Hurston:

> "There came a time," Hurston writes, "as indicated by the length of the affair and her boldness, that she no longer lived in Live Oak, nor yet the United States. Her permanent address was Dr. C. LeRoy Adams. It was a phase of life mounted on granite. The horizon of her world had no gate.[111]

Hurston's actual statement reads:

> Ruby was a woman who was used to getting her way about things. Sam had hurt her, so there was no longer any mingling blood. Then there came the temptation of opportunity in the person of the handsome and dynamic Dr. Adams. So there came a time….

To make her point, Evans has to omit any mention of Ruby's "getting her way about things," of Sam's having "hurt her," or of the "temptation" of Adams. Moreover, she fails to explore Hurston's reference to McCollum's "boldness," or Hurston's full depiction of McCollum's attraction to Adams: "She was a woman terribly in love, and with us females, that makes strange and terrible creatures of us."[112]

These omissions are highly misleading for the purpose of establishing a premise.

From Hurston's account, McCollum adored Adams and boldly ran after him to see him at his office daily even when he was trying to distance himself from her.

In short, Ruby McCollum could not accept rejection.

It is apparent that what Hurston is describing is obsessive love—a state in which one person feels an overwhelming obsessive desire to possess someone they feel a strong attraction to, combined with an inability to accept failure or rejection. But obsessive love has nothing to do with being "colonized."

Evans then notes that Ruby McCollum ended one of her letters with "I am Ruby McCollum," and cites this as her "writing the body." She then cites a study about women who have been abused in a patriarchal society, reclaiming their bodies through affirmative statements.[113]

In fact, McCollum's first use of "I am Ruby McCollum" is when she writes, "Regardless of color, I am Ruby McCollum."[114] Here, McCollum is making a bold statement of her personhood and her desire to have a fair trial, regardless of the color of her skin—not reclaiming herself from Adams's "colonization." And it is much more likely that she is reiterating this sentiment in the continued use of the "I am Ruby McCollum" closing to her letters.

Evans then refers to a work of literary theory, *The Madwoman in the Attic*, by Gilbert and Gubar, to conclude, "Patriarchal civilization makes women sick, both physically and mentally. Ruby McCollum's aches and pains had no medical cause."[115]

But *The Madwoman in the Attic* is not by any stretch a medical study that offers proof that women are made sick mentally and physically by patriarchal civilizations. Rather, it is a work of literary analysis that explores a trope, commonly found in nineteenth-century literature, when the mentally ill (at least in England) were referred to as "mad." In fact, Gilbert and Gubar proposed that all female characters in novels by men of this period can be categorized as either angel or monster. They also proposed that nineteenth-century female writers carried quite a bit of rage and frustration about the misogynistic world they lived in, and that this rage was depicted through the figure of the madwoman in the attic in novels by women of the same period.

After dismissing any medical reason for McCollum's vague aches and pains and comparing her to women in Victorian novels, Evans continues her argument that McCollum was being "colonized," by referring to a study by Alice Bullard on French colonization of North Africa in the early 1800s. After introducing the study, Evans concludes, "The reactions of these North African women, whom Bullard calls 'the detritus of the colonial process,' are similar to those of McCollum."[116]

But Bullard's study, "The Truth in Madness," actually states:

> The detritus of the colonial process, incapable of sustaining the demands of
> French or local culture, outside of both, they provide a question, a criticism,
> and a window onto the forces that fail to be ordered or repressed by reason.[117]

Evans omits Bullard's contention that this "detritus of the colonial process" came about from the dual demands of French colonialism *and* local culture.

In fact, Bullard's study explores the complex superimposition of French medical practice onto the indigenous culture's religious interpretation of madness:

> Arabs, Berbers, and other North Africans perceived individuals with
> deranged or altered psychic states as affected by the sacred. The veil of modern
> psychiatry made these phenomena appear to French doctors as mental
> pathologies; what the French called "mental alienation," appeared to North

Africans as some variant of a divine possession or perhaps the outcome of a magical curse.[118]

This belief that madness is caused by spirit possession was not unique to this area of the world but can be read in the New Testament in accounts of Jesus exorcising demons and casting them into swine.

Bullard cites several studies to report that during their colonization of North Africa in the early 1800s, the horrified French witnessed the insane inhabiting the public byways and being available for those who sought their blessings, usually through coveted sexual intercourse with the insane as a saintly or purifying act.[119]

Bullard's otherwise quite interesting study is flawed by her confirmation bias in utterly disregarding one of the primary contributors to "madness" during this period in history, as described by Andrea Schull in *Madness in Civilization: A Cultural History of Insanity from the Bible to Freud, from the Madhouse to Modern Medicine:*

> Syphilis (Pat. 25), for example, was brought back to Europe at the very end of the fifteenth century by Columbus's crew and later would contribute mightily to the population of asylums in the nineteenth and twentieth centuries. When it arrived in Europe, the English promptly dubbed it the French disease. The French, whose army had contracted the disease in great numbers while laying siege to Naples (and whose mercenaries then helped to spread the pox all across Europe), preferred to call it the Neapolitan disease.[120]

It is difficult to imagine Bullard being unaware of the contribution of syphilis to increasing the population of the mentally ill during this period in European history, and especially difficult to understand why she would ignore it entirely when soldiers in the French army, deployed to colonize certain areas of Africa, were heavily infected with the disease and encountered "mad" women in the streets who were accustomed to casual sexual encounters.

Despite Bullard's error in failing to address the contribution of syphilis to the "madness" of prostitutes in an area colonized by the French, it is important to continue an analysis of her article to understand Evans's confirmation bias in citing it.

In 1838, the French passed a national law, applicable in France as well as its colonies, confining the mad to asylums. They further envisioned that these new asylums should be run by doctors and that patients would receive humane, therapeutic treatments from medical experts.[121]

From a presentist point of view, the French acted humanely. But from the perspective of the indigenous population, the stress of institutionalization by a foreign invader, who did not speak the native language and who imposed different cultural practices, merely added another layer to the problem of mental health, compounding the stressors that the mentally ill had been experiencing in their precolonial culture. Bullard writes:

> The combination of a secularized understanding of madness with the emphasis on internment in French-run institutions effectively cordoned North Africans off from their own culture, from indigenous remedies and—since French doctors in the nineteenth century rarely knew Arabic—from communication with their doctors.[122]

Evans minimizes this more complex analysis, which attributes the suffering of psychotic women to both local culture and French colonialism preferring the more simplistic explanation that the stress of colonization caused an increased incidence in mental illness among women.

It is only by minimizing the contribution of local culture to these women's plight that Evans can make her point regarding the "colonizing" of McCollum. Evans holds on to the concept of colonizing for later use, in comparing McCollum to these colonized African women: "Both were victims of violent acts of colonization and patriarchy; both exhibited symptoms of madness, and both were closeted away without serious consideration of how the first act may have informed behavior that society viewed as symptomatic of the second."[123]

Equally important is the fact that Evans's comparison of what is considered "symptoms of madness" across cultures and timelines—the segregationist US South in the mid-1900s versus colonized North Africa in the early 1800s—conflicts with sound psychiatric principles and diagnostic practices.

In particular, Evans fails to consider differing classification systems of French versus American psychiatric practice; differing ways that different cultures express, experience, and cope with feelings of distress; and differing relationships between culture-specific diagnoses and mood disorders—defined in the glossary of DSM-V as "culture-bound syndrome."

First, diagnostic classifications of symptoms and diseases as set forth in the American psychiatry's DSM vary significantly from diagnostic classifications of symptoms and diseases in the parallel French diagnostic and statistical manual, the CFTMEA (*Classification Francaise de Troubles Mentaux d'Enfants et d'Adolescent*), as does the history of French versus American psychiatry before the establishment of these diagnostic systems.

In discussing cross-cultural differences in psychiatric practice while limiting his discussion to the single diagnosis of ADHD, Manuel Vallee maintains that the DSM and CFTMEA differ in three significant ways:

(1) Theoretical orientation (biological versus psychodynamic), (2) the view that symptoms should be counted as opposed to understood, and (3) the presence versus absence of symptom checklists. These differences have significant implications for the clinical encounter because they lead to very different conceptualizations of mental illness. In particular, where French clinicians tend to see mental problems as resulting from psychological and social problems, American clinicians are encouraged to assume that the problem lies at the biological level.[124]

A National Institutes of Health study says this about cultural differences in expression of symptoms:

Idioms of distress are ways in which different cultures experience, express, and cope with feelings of distress. One example is *somatization,* or the expression of distress through physical symptoms (Kirmayer and Young 1998). Stomach disturbances, excessive gas, palpitations, and chest pain are common forms of somatization among Puerto Ricans, Mexican-Americans, and whites (Escobar et al. 1987). Some Asian groups express more cardiopulmonary and vestibular symptoms, such as dizziness, vertigo, and blurred vision (Hsu and Folstein 1997). In Africa and South Asia, somatization sometimes takes the form of burning hands and feet, or the experience of "worms in the head" or "ants" crawling under the skin (APA, 1994).[125]

Wolfgang Jilek discusses transcultural psychiatry with respect to schizophrenic psychoses:

In recent decades the influence of culture on symptom profiles, course and outcome of schizophrenic disorders has been demonstrated in systematic comparative research. Most prominent were the international collaborative research projects undertaken by the Mental Health Division of WHO, the International Pilot Study of Schizophrenia (IPSS) and the study of the Determinants of Outcome of Severe Mental Disorders (DOSMED). These studies confirmed that the syndrome originally described by Emil Kraepelin and Eugen Bleuler (KRAEPELIN 1896, BLEULER 1922) exists in very diverse ethnic and cultural groups. However, the studies also revealed that pathoplastic, i.e., illness-shaping, effects of socio-cultural factors are co-determinants of form, course and final outcome of schizophrenic disorders. Pathoplastic effects of socio-cultural factors appear to shape the symptom profiles manifested by sufferers from schizophrenia differently in developed and developing countries. Schizophrenic patients in Western developed countries showed a high frequency of depressive symptoms, primary delusions, thought insertion and thought broadcasting, while in non-Western developing countries visual and directed auditory hallucinations were most frequent (SARTORIUS et al. 1986, JABLENSKY et al. 1992).[126]

Guarnaccia and Pincay, in an article investigating the relationship between culture-specific diagnoses and mood disorders, cite the following description of the diagnosis of *ataque de nervios* (attack of nerves) among Puerto Ricans and other Caribbean Latinos:

> Commonly reported symptoms include uncontrollable shouting, attacks of crying, trembling, heat in the chest rising into the head, and verbal or physical aggression. Dissociative experiences, seizurelike or fainting episodes, and suicidal gestures are prominent in some attacks but absent in others. A general feature of an *ataque de nervios* is a sense of being out of control. *Ataques de nervios* frequently occur as a direct result of a stressful event relating to the family (e.g. news of a death of a close relative, a separation or divorce from a spouse, conflicts with a spouse or children, or witnessing an accident involving a family member). People may experience amnesia for what occurred during the *ataque de nervios*, but they otherwise return rapidly to their usual level of functioning. Although descriptions of some *ataques de nervios* most closely fit the DSM-IV description of panic attacks, the association of most *ataques* with a precipitating event and the frequent absence of the hallmark symptom of acute fear or apprehension distinguish them from panic disorder.[127]

Alarcon expresses this more succinctly: "Culture impregnates every clinical and non-clinical even in any and all diseases."[128]

Evans's failure to take into account cross-cultural differences in two disparate systems of diagnostic practices and in French and American diagnostic manuals; her failure to consider idioms of distress, which account for differing manifestations of clinical symptoms for what may be identical mental illnesses; her failure to account for culture-specific diagnoses; and her failure to cite sources attributing the surge of ill-defined symptoms among women resulting from rampant syphilis spread by colonizing French soldiers after the reign of Napoleon to dramatic rises in institutionalization of the mentally ill—all conspire to invalidate any comparison between Ruby McCollum and colonized North African women.

In short, Ruby McCollum cannot be compared to a character in a nineteenth-century novel or to North African women colonized by the French in the early 1800s.

Evans uses fallacious reasoning to support her confirmation bias that Ruby McCollum was "colonized," while failing to consider cultural mores and laws that suppressed women in the American South of the 1950s, especially by ignoring domestic abuse.

It is also true that when women suffering from these stressors went to the doctor to complain of various aches and pains that we now know can result in somatoform disorders—such as fibromyalgia—physicians labeled them "hypochondriacal" and "hysterical," continuing a long tradition beginning with the ancient Greeks and continuing until the 1980s, when "hysteria" was omitted from the DSM-III.

But Evans dismisses any physical dimension to McCollum's vague aches and pains, declaring that her symptoms "had no medical cause."[129] A fairer assessment would be that McCollum's indefinite aches and pains had no medical cause that could be determined by her doctors in 1952. The difference is that medicine in the early 1950s was ill equipped to diagnose a host of vague aches and pains that do in fact have a physical cause. Thus, McCollum may very well have been suffering from some physical ailment, possibly exacerbated by physical and mental abuse.

Adams functioned well in this environment. He was abusive, as his crony Jeff Elliott testified, saying that Adams had a "hot temper" and that he had seen Adams slap his white girlfriend so hard that he would "spin her around like a top."[130] According to Edith Park, the hospital nurse anesthetist, Adams also yelled viciously and hurled obscenities at Ms. Sheffield, the head nurse at the hospital, to the point that she sobbed the rest of the day.[131] It is notable that both of these victims of Adams's abuse were *white* females.

Within this context, Ruby McCollum, who was also slapped around by her husband, had a difficult time maintaining the control that she desired in her relationships. By all accounts, she was well educated, proud, even arrogant, which did not square with the Southern feminine ideal in the 1950s—especially for a black woman.

Moreover, it is not necessary to resort to exotic and convoluted theories to explain Ruby McCollum's abusive and dysfunctional ménage à trois when she had a husband who cheated on her and had distanced himself from her after she had a "white" baby by Adams, a lover who was becoming increasingly abusive and pulling away from her while taking more and more of her money, and a pregnancy that she did not want, with one man threatening to kill her if she had an abortion and the other threatening to kill her if she did not. To top it off, a recently enacted federal law required her husband to declare openly that he ran a gambling operation that was still illegal both in the county as well as the state, and to surrender his accounting records to the feds upon demand to pay taxes. Certainly, business would fall off dramatically if the names of local law enforcement members who received money as payoffs had to be recorded, and profits would plummet if the McCollums stopped recording those names and then had to pay taxes on the cash payouts as if they had kept the cash themselves.

Evans could have chosen to investigate McCollum's vague aches and pains within the context of a woman suffering from the foregoing stressors. Doing so might have led her to explore several possible diagnoses, including fibromyalgia.

Instead, to advance the a priori conclusion that McCollum's problems resulted from her being "colonized" by Adams, Evans chooses the anachronistic and anatopic plights of women over a century earlier in obscure Victorian novel tropes and syphilis-infected French-colonized North African street prostitutes experiencing a culturally sanctioned religious experience.

Simply put, she is looking in both the wrong time and the wrong place to make her point.

Confirmation bias and Ruby McCollum's Power and Wealth

A narrator's voiceover in "The Shot Doctor" episode in *A Crime to Remember* asks, "What does it mean to have power when that power can be taken away in the blink of an eye?" The documentary's producers give an unbalanced portrayal of the murder. Otherwise, they would have acknowledged the very real taking away of power, "in the blink of an eye," that happened to the murder victim, Dr. Adams.

Ruby McCollum was far from being robbed of her power—the power that kept her alive even after she had murdered the most beloved and powerful white man in Suwannee County.

Ruby McCollum's power lay partly in being able to afford a dream team of attorneys who eventually overturned her death sentence. Against a barrage of objections by the prosecution, she was allowed to speak of Adams's forcing sex on her, forcing her to have his child, and physically abusing her. Her testimony was groundbreaking at the time, being the first testimony of a woman of color charged with murdering a white man who forced her to have his children.

Ruby McCollum also had the power of a wealthy extended family in her brother-in-law, Buck McCollum, who had run bolita in the more populous city of Ft. Myers for years before Sam and Ruby set up business in Live Oak. Buck McCollum was the original banker who set his brother and sister-in-law up in business, and it is apparent from Ruby McCollum's letters that he helped call the shots with the attorneys.

Finally, and most significantly, she had the power of her little black accounting book, which contained the names of many local white people who—having participated in the McCollum business of organized crime and political corruption—would spend years behind bars should their involvement be revealed to the IRS team scouring the town after the murder.

So, despite the asymmetry in her relationship with Adams, there is no doubt that Ruby McCollum, through her wealth, retained power even while in jail. Indeed, her trial was a landmark in the segregationist South.

Regarding the McCollum wealth, Huie reports that Sam Jr. and his uncle, Buck McCollum, met to transfer the cash that Sam McCollum had fled town with after the murder, and that Buck McCollum had told Sam Jr. that he was placing the money in a Tampa bank for safekeeping. Huie also reports that Sam Jr. said that this was not all of his father's money.[132] After this encounter, Jeff Elliott found $47,500 in a bank in Tampa—which the court recovered and placed in probate.[133]

Sam Jr. was later found wandering around Live Oak with a suitcase filled with $80,000 in cash, which he was made to deposit in a local bank.

Huie gives no explanation of how Sam Jr. acquired this money, but he continued to run the family business after his father died. He went to prison for tax evasion in 1975, and the FBI confiscated $250,000 in cash from his house when he was arrested. It was returned, minus taxes, upon his release from prison.[134]

Huie notes that by 1953, payments to lawyers totaled $36,000: $13,000 to Cannon; $8,000 to McGriff; $6,000 to Blackwell; $5,000 to Crews; $3,000 to Cogdill; and $1,000 to Henderson. This does not account for cash payments early on to Pigeye Crews for $2,500 and to John Cogdill for $3,000.[135] Huie also notes that $1,800 disappeared from McCollum's purse when she was arrested, and that another $10,000 disappeared from her bank accounts.[136]

Huie reports that in probate, the McCollum estate was valued at $135,000, of which Ruby's "child's" portion came to about $27,000, leaving $108,000 for the McCollum children. This did not include the value of the McCollum home, which was appraised at $20,000 and was in the name of Sam McCollum.[137] Against Ruby McCollum's $27,000 share of the estate, Cannon had filed a preprobate claim of $10,000 for additional attorney's fees, and McGriff had filed a claim of $8,000. These claims, if given priority, would leave only $9,000 in Ruby McCollum's share of the estate, against which Mrs. Adams could exercise her claim for $85,000 for the wrongful death of her husband.[138] The court awarded attorney Blackwell $6,000 for handling the probate, and Jeff Elliott a $200 finder's fee for tracking down the $47,500 of McCollum money in the Tampa bank.[139]

The amount of McCollum cash found floating around after Sam McCollum's death is all the more impressive considering that US Census data reports that the median gross annual wage in 1952 was around $4,000.[140] In Suwannee County, where most wage earners in 1952 worked on farms for fifty cents an hour, the median wage was significantly lower than this.

It can be argued that the McCollums were worth quite a bit more than could be tracked by bank accounts, landholdings, and cash. After all, "cash money," as US Treasury agents well know, is exceedingly difficult to trace.

What cannot be argued is that the cash and landholdings that were recovered were distributed equitably according to the laws of the time, and that $108,000—a significant portion of what remained after legal expenses—was set aside for the care of the McCollum children.

Finally, William Huie paid the McCollum estate $40,000 for the rights to portray Ruby in a movie he planned to produce, and the funds were placed in a special trust fund for Ruby McCollum during her last twenty years of life.[141] (The screenplay that Huie commissioned never made it to the silver screen, and now rests in peace in the Huie Collection at the Ohio State University library in Columbus—which is where it will always remain since it is a vainglorious account of Huie's alleged rescue of an abused and helpless colored woman in the South).

With all this wealth under her control, there are indications that Ruby McCollum was accustomed to bribing officials and that she expected special treatment—and even release—through bribes:

1. At the trial, Deputy Gray testified regarding a private talk he had with Ruby McCollum in an upstairs bathroom of her home when she was arrested. After testifying that she confessed to the murder and told him she did not know why she shot Adams, Gray reports that she pointed out the murder weapon in the bamboo hedge outside her bathroom window. He continues (emphasis added):

    A.   After she did that, I say, "Ruby, do you realize that you have killed one of the most important men in the county?" I says, **"Now, I am an officer, and it is my duty to protect you, but you will have to do as I say do." And she says, "Well, I don't want to leave now because there is no one to stay with my children." And I said, "Your children will be all right, Ruby."** And we turned around and went downstairs, and when I got down to the bottom of the stairs, I pointed to the Sheriff and nodded and said that she was the one; that she had told me she had shot Dr. Adams, and he taken her in custody.[142]

There is no mention of money when the prosecutor questions him. But during cross-examination, Ruby McCollum's attorney, Frank Cannon, asks Gray (emphasis added):

Q.   Did you know her husband, Sam?

A.   Yes, Sir.

Q.   How long have you known him?

A.   Approximately 3 or 4 years.

Q.   **Did you see any brown pocketbook there anywhere?**

A.   **That morning?**

Q.   **Yes.**

A.   **No, I didn't notice any brown pocketbook.**

Q.   **Did you go through any of the articles in the house?**

A.   **That morning, no.**

Q.   **Later on in the day?**

A.   **No, Sir.**

Q.   **Did you go back there?**

MR. EDWARDS: That is not proper cross—at some other time or on some other date.

THE COURT: Sustained.

Q.   How long did you stay there?

A.   That morning?

Q.   Yes.

A.   Approximately 30 minutes, possibly. I was that long in the house. I didn't go back in the house after I came out when Ruby came out. I didn't go back in the house any more. I went around to the back of the house and went to looking for the gun.

Q.   **Now, have you related all of the conversations that you have had with the Defendant since August 3?**

MR. EDWARDS: That is not a proper question. We only questioned him about the conversation that took place in the bathroom in the home of the Defendant right at that time. It is not proper cross.

THE COURT: Objection sustained.

Q.   **Have you related in its entirety all of the conversation you had with her on August 3?**

A.   Yes, Sir.

Q.   Have you talked with her since that time?

MR. EDWARDS: That is irrelevant and immaterial and not in proper cross.

THE COURT: Has he talked with her since that time?

MR. CANNON: Yes, Sir.

THE COURT: Objection sustained.[143]

First, Cannon establishes that Deputy Gray knew Sam McCollum. Cannon then asks the deputy five questions related to his knowing about or looking for Ruby McCollum's purse, which he knew from conversations with Ruby had contained $1,800 in cash when it was last in her possession. The next two questions concern whether Deputy Gray has revealed the full extent of the conversation he had with her. Gray stated that he did. The third question concerns whether Deputy Gray and Ruby McCollum spoke after the arrest, but the prosecution's objection to the question is sustained.

This line of questioning by Frank Cannon strongly suggests that Ruby McCollum had told him that Deputy Gray knew Sam McCollum, as she would later testify, that the deputy knew about the money in her purse, that the deputy had failed to relate the entire conversation that he had with her, and that the deputy continued to speak with her after her arrest.

2.   During her testimony at trial, Ruby McCollum gives her account of her conversation with Gray in the bathroom (emphasis added):

> I walked upstairs, and he came up behind me and he told me, he said, "Ruby, I know your husband. **I know Sam and I have been doing quite a few things for him,** and I want you to tell me where is the gun." He sat there a while and said, "I want to know who Sam's wife is." I didn't say anything for a while, and then he said, "**I am here to protect you.** Tell me where the gun is and where is Sam's wife." I said, "The gun is out there on the back." Then someone opened the bathroom door and they told me to come on, and he told me to go ahead on with them, and **I told him, "I wanted somebody with my children," and he said, "The children will be all right."** I said, "I want somebody to see about my children," and I called my big girl and told her and Sonja and the baby to stay there, and told her to see about the little girls and I went with the officers.[144]

McCollum establishes that the deputy spoke with her privately, away from other members of law enforcement, that the deputy worked for her husband, that he said that he was there to protect her, and that she asked him to protect her children.

The fact that Ruby McCollum asked Deputy Gray to speak with her privately and that he agreed is highly irregular and indicates that she expected special treatment. It is also highly suspicious that Deputy Gray, who knew full well who she was, asked her where Sam's wife was, giving her a chance to deny that she was Ruby McCollum. Whether this was intended to allow her to escape and go up North to stay with relatives will never be known, but it is one possibility that has not been discussed elsewhere.

Further evidence that McCollum was continuing to speak with law enforcement after her arrest appears in her third letter from the Suwannee County Jail, in which she stated, "I told her the sheriff told me not to take needles." ("Her" refers to a nurse at Raiford.)[145]

3. McCollum wrote this letter to P. Guy Crews from Suwannee County Jail, about a conversation regarding a payment to influence the outcome of the trial (emphasis added):

> Mr. Cogdill was over here Thursday evening ask when had I saw you I said Monday. He said he talked to you Wednesday night & yesterday morning. Then he said he wanted to get my people together if I would give him a note to give Buck. **He wants the rest of his money if he can get it. I told him Buck wasn't going to pay him all of it now no way. He said you know I can have this thing set up or reversed. I didn't say anything.** He also something about a phyciatrist [sic]. Then he wanted to know if I got along as good here as did in Raiford. I said I don't know.
>
> He told **Lawyer Blackwell who helped Sam in his no. business** etc. That I had a baby for Dr. And gona have another one for him. He had another man with him said his name is Mr. Carson from there, this man said Cogdill is the best Ruby I didn't say anything I just want you to know what's happening. **He said the Judge Adams was the only one on his side. Kept saying he needed some money now. So if you need any extra money to get everything going your way let me know.**[146]

When she writes, "If you need any extra money to get everything going your way let me know," it is evident that McCollum believed that money could help buy her way out of her predicament.

4. McCollum wrote this letter to Huie on May 25, 1954, asking him to "bail" her out of the Suwannee County Jail:

> Dear Mr. Huie,
>
> Please get me a cash bond or have me turned out of this place (free). Please do that as quick as possible.
>
> I am
> Ruby McCollum[147]

5. Though arrested and tried for murder, McCollum is never made to undergo a "perp walk" or to wear prison garb.

    There is not a single photograph of Ruby McCollum escorted in handcuffs before, during, or after her trial. Nor is there a single photograph of her wearing prison garb. In fact, even the photo of McCollum that was taken by her family with the consent of the jailer in the Suwannee County Jail and used by Evans on the cover of her book shows McCollum wearing a modest dress, not prison garb.[148]

    This is proof of the special treatment that she received as a prisoner while in Suwannee County, from the moment she was arrested to the moment she was sent to the Chattahoochee State Mental Hospital, two years later.

Confirmation Bias and Live Oak's "Silencing" of the Story

In her book *The Silencing of Ruby McCollum*, Evans laments the silencing of Ruby McCollum, referring primarily to the gag order that Judge Adams placed on her preventing her from speaking with the press, the number of objections by the prosecution that were sustained during McCollum's testimony at her trial, and the town's supposed unanimous agreement that the motive was an argument over her doctor bill.

But Evans fails to mention one of McCollum's letters, written from the Suwannee County Jail, referring to her stay at Raiford, in which she wrote that she was visited by a news editor from a Jacksonville paper yet refused to talk with him: "After you became my lawyer a News Editor from Jaxville Melson he said came in and ask two or three question[s.] Is the Dr. you baby's father? I said I don't care to talk."[149]

Evidently, when visited by a reporter shortly after her arrest, she chose of her own free will to remain silent. This gives an entirely different perspective on Judge Adams's gag order and the effect that it had on preventing Ruby McCollum from speaking to the press. It is apparent that she either did not care to talk, or had agreed with her attorneys that it would be in her best interest not to talk.

Regarding Evans's account of the town's collusion in fabricating a story that an argument over a doctor bill led to a murder, there was no need to fabricate such a story since Ruby McCollum, along with several other witnesses, testified to this during her trial. The following is a portion of McCollum's testimony concerning discussion of the bill, in response to her attorney Frank Cannon's questioning:

> A. Then I asked him: "Doctor, I owe you for two calls, don't I," and he said, "Yes, and this one will make three." I said, "That will make three." I gave him ten dollars and he gave me back one dollar, and I put the money in my bag. Then I thought about the bill. When he came back, I said, "Dr. Adams, a bill came out to the house for Sam for $116."
>
> Q. Who is Sam?
>
> A. My husband.
>
> Q. Go ahead.
>
> A. He said, "Yes, I am going to get my money, too, if I have to turn him over to the county judge." So I said, "I have $100 I want to pay on it. May I peep and see who made that bill?" and he said to see Thelma about that. I said, "That is all right, just give me a receipt for it, please." I said, "Then I will owe you how much?" And he said, "Ten dollars," and I said, "OK" I said, "I will bring it back sometime when I come in next week," and he said that would be all right. Where we were at that time I was leaning on that table in the back.[150]

It is clear that there was at least a discussion of a doctor bill, which might be characterized as an "argument" to the extent that Adams is quoted as saying, "Yes, I am going to get my money, too, if I have to turn him over to the county judge."

The town need look no further than McCollum's own testimony to believe that an argument over a doctor bill was at least one possible motive for the murder, although anyone who knew the McCollums had to know that this was not credible since the McCollums always paid their bills.

Regarding the story of an argument over a doctor bill, Releford McGriff offers the following reason for the argument over the bill (emphasis added):

She went in there with her mind made up, and she knew that she had to trick him into turning his back to her in order to get the gun out of that bag. Her crazed mind knew that much. She was too small and he was too big. In one of those small treatment rooms, she knew that with him looking at her she'd never have a chance to get the **gun out before he overpowered her. I think her crazed mind figured out, maybe with some satisfaction, that the way to make him turn his back was to hand him a hundred-dollar bill and ask for a receipt. Maybe she planned for him to die with the hundred-dollar bill in one hand and the fountain pen in the other.**[151]

No one in Live Oak, including McGriff, believed the story of the fight over a doctor bill, since everyone knew that not only were the McCollums wealthy, and Ruby McCollum was prompt in paying the family bills.

Instead, according to her own attorney, Ruby McCollum planned ahead to create this scenario to get Adams to turn his back and write a receipt, giving her an opportunity to shoot him. As McGriff said, "She was too small and he was too big" for her to get her gun out of her handbag without him having a chance to defend himself. And since he had a foot and over a hundred pounds on her, the outcome of a direct approach was predictable.

While ignoring McCollum's role in creating the story of the fight over a doctor bill, Evans also has to ignore these contemporary accounts to support her thesis of a "conspiracy of silence."

In fact, the motive of the doctor bill, created by Ruby McCollum herself, furnished an explanation for an otherwise senseless murder.

And in proposing that the town silenced the story of Ruby McCollum, Evans fails to consider Huie's account of the IRS's role in sealing the lips of its residents:

> Letters were written to insurance companies and also to banks, inquiring for boxes
> rented under variations of the name Clifford LeRoy Adams, Jr. The Bureau of Internal
> Revenue joined the search.[152]

Aside from the audit of Adams's accounts and records, the IRS soon expanded its search to look into bolita and to find anyone who had not registered under the federal gambling legislation of 1951.

The citizens of Live Oak were terrified that Ruby's little black book might find its way into the hands of these federal agents, resulting in fines and imprisonment.

The question in the current discussion of confirmation bias is why Evans failed to mention a single word about the IRS's role in silencing the town. The only reasonable conclusion is that failing to do so suited her purpose.

It is also apparent to anyone who has researched Huie's papers, archived at the University of Ohio at Columbus, that the citizens of Live Oak had much to hide besides Adams's affair with Ruby, or their unpaid taxes on gambling earnings.

For example, Edith Park, the hospital nurse anesthetist and employee of Dr. Sims and then Dr. Adams, had much to say about the hidden affairs of nurses and doctors at Suwannee County Hospital. Her letters to Huie, reproduced in Appendix A, are filled with accounts of illicit sex, substance abuse, and questionable medical practices, including abortions at a time when abortions were illegal.

In 1952, probably no small town would have welcomed scrutiny of such reprobate behavior among its medical personnel—people who were highly educated, affluent, deacons in their churches and leaders in their community.

As William Huie reports, when he confronted Judge Adams regarding Ruby McCollum's First Amendment Rights, the jurist expressed this most eloquently:

> "Huie," he said, "I've been very careful to try to protect this community from embarrassment. I don't want a dead man smeared. I don't want this case commercialized or sensationalized. I want it ended in a quiet, orderly manner. I don't want to see anything go wrong."[153]

Judge Adams was undoubtedly aware of the sins of his fellow citizens in Live Oak and that he feared exposure in the press. In this regard, he was no different from any other judge, in any other community in the United States at the time, who did not want the underbelly of his town exposed for all to see, and a murder case tried in the press.

Where Judge Adams differed from other judges, even in his time, was in his abrogation of Ruby McCollum's First Amendment Rights, and that is what fueled Huie's crusade against him.

The irony here is that even without a gag order, Ruby McCollum may very well have refused to talk with the press. She had, after all, refused to speak with the Jacksonville reporter who tried to interview her in Raiford.[154]

As for her writing Huie about wanting to tell him her whole story, that was sometime later, in a letter written on May 23, 1954—well after her trial. Besides, McCollum had managed to get out letters to her attorneys damaging to Adams before her first trial, so there is little reason to believe that she could not have conveyed anything she had to say to him if she wanted.[155]

What is also overlooked in all the recent renderings of the story is that William Huie used his contempt hearing to tell the whole sordid backstory of the case. In a headline article appearing in the *Pittsburgh Courier* on October 23, 1954, the unknown reporter announces, "Huie Gets Ruby's Story on Record; Free on Bail."[156]

While Huie never succeeded in having the gag order on McCollum lifted, he was allowed to fully and completely tell her side of the story for all to hear. He also implicated Black and was later vindicated when the federal government indicted Black on racketeering charges. Ironically, Huie was allowed to testify without being silenced, since the court needed his testimony to support the contempt charge.

Huie's strategy had prevailed. He had made McCollum's story front-page news in the *Pittsburgh Currier* and preserved the record for posterity.

Confirmation Bias and Ruby McCollum's Psychiatric Diagnoses.

At the time of her first psychiatric admission by Adams, McCollum was addicted to something that Adams had given her, as witnessed by one of the Brewster Hospital nurses interviewed by William Huie.[157] It seems that the hospital staff could not get the pouch containing the drug away from her, and when she had used it up, she demanded to be released. It is difficult to understand, however, how the staff could not confiscate the pouch, since staff members had said that she was given intensive insulin shock therapy, during which it would have been easy enough to confiscate the pouch and analyze its contents.

In the second year of her incarceration in the Suwannee County jail, prior to her appeal of her death sentence, Ruby's attorneys were again raising questions about her mental capacity to understand her rights during her appeal. While there is no record of exact conversations that would have led them to this conclusion, there is evidence that she was undergoing some form of mental deterioration after two years of confinement.

The first piece of evidence is a power of attorney dated August 19, 1954 shown on the next page.[167] This power of attorney gives William Huie the right to collect money on her behalf in his efforts to publicize her plight, without any supervision of how he would spend the funds.

Scrawled across the bottom of the power of attorney, in Ruby McCollum's handwriting, are these instructions: "Please disregard such as this copy. I did not give no one any permission to draw up any such papers." The fact that she wrote this and mailed it back to Huie demonstrates that she did not want to sign a power of attorney allowing anyone to control money collected on her behalf.

Live Oak, Florida

August 19th, 1954

POWER OF ATTORNEY.

The undersigned Ruby McCollum hereby gives to Hon. William Bradford Huie full power of attorney in fact to act for her and in her stead in and about soliciting, collecting and raising funds for her defense in the criminal prosecution now pending against her, and procure the assistance of any individual, publication, organization, association, corporation or other person in soliciting and collecting funds for the defense of the undersigned, and to ~~disbuse~~ disburse any and all funds collected as he may see fit in the defense of the undersigned Ruby McCollum and in publicity of her cause.

In witness whereof I have hereunto set my hand and seal this 19th day of August 1954.

WITNESS: RUBY MCCOLLUM

~~Please [illegible]~~
~~by this copy!~~
Please desire and send me the copy.
I did not give my any permission to draw up any such Papers.

Figure 8: Power of Attorney drafted by William Huie

It is probable that Ruby had access to Huie's frequent articles in the *Courier* since her brother, Matt visited her frequently and subscribed to the paper. In those articles, Huie promoted himself as a defender of her First Amendment Rights, and poor mouthed how much of his own money he had spent in doing so. As a result, the newspaper reported that thousands of readers sent dollar bills in envelopes mailed to him care of the *Courier.* There was never any accounting for this money, and this may or may not have concerned Ruby—who was accustomed to keeping the books for her husband's gambling and liquor business—to the extent that she was unwilling to sign the power of attorney.

Even if this is speculation, the clarity of thinking in refusing to sign a legal document that was not drafted or reviewed by her attorneys speaks to her sanity.

On the other hand, the document also reveals her rapidly deteriorating handwriting. Notice that there is the faint trace of her "Please disregard" admonition that appears to have been erased, and then a second reiteration of the same statement is written over it. Finally, a third attempt is made, with the exact wording, written below the first two attempts.

While it is not possible to determine why it took her three attempts to successfully hand write two short sentences, it is apparent that she was having difficulty putting pen to paper. One possible explanation for this difficulty is that she was suffering from "intention tremor," a condition that only appears when a person is performing a highly skilled, goal-oriented task, such as handwriting.

The causes of intention tremor are legion, but, ruling out Parkinsonism, psychotropic drugs and extreme stress are front runners among the possibilities. This said, she was undoubtedly stressed by her incarceration and her belief that she was being poisoned as she told her attorneys on many occasions.

As to the possible effect of psychotropics, she was medicated while in the mental ward at Brewster, and claims that she was given "shots" while incarcerated at Raiford, but there is no extant record of which medications were given at Brewster or at Raiford. (More on this in the next section discussing her self-reported medications.)

Another instance of deteriorating handwriting that should be considered in assessing McCollum's state of mind is a letter that she wrote on September 1, 1954.

Mr. Huie,

Please handle my case. I tried those lawyers it is too much confusion between them.
And it is really harmful to me.

I am
Ruby McCollum[158]

This is the fourth in a series of letters that Ruby McCollum closes with "I am Ruby," or "I am Ruby McCollum." The signature in this letter is not as carefully crafted as her signatures before or after. The handwriting is not as crisp, and the two small strokes that she usually places below the lowercase "c" in "McCollum," elevating the letter to the level of the uppercase "C," are not present. In fact, the first "c" is crowded against the second, and the "I am" and the signature

overlap. She also adds her middle initial, "M," and the "R" in "Ruby" is now executed with different strokes. Both signatures have the final period.

Aside from the deteriorating handwriting, it is curious that Ruby did not trust Huie enough to sign a power of attorney to him on a document dated August 19, yet less than a month later she trusted Huie more than her own attorneys and asked him to represent her. It is possible that in her mental confusion she thought that Huie was an attorney, when he was not.

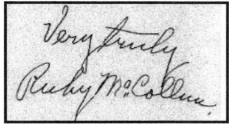

Figure 9: Usual Signature

Figure 10: Signature of Sept. 1, 1954[161]

Several weeks later, on September 21, 1954, Dr. M. C. Moore, a psychiatrist, diagnosed Ruby with delusional behavior in his report to the court:

> On the day of my examination, I found her in a filthy, foul-smelling jail cell, lying on a cot without mattress with her entire body, including her head, covered with an old Army blanket. Scattered around the bed were many cans of food, also refuse. Most of the odor was due to her own physical uncleanliness. With her brother present, many attempts were made to converse with her but failed to elicit any response other than peeking from under the blanket on 2 occasions. The more she became aware of someone present, the more she continued a constant agitation-like attempt to pull the blanket tighter and more secure around her body. At no time did she lie perfectly still. After some time, the blanket was forcibly removed from her head and she struck at the examining physician. The blanket was kept from her head forcibly for a period of time and she was questioned. There was no verbal or emotional response to my questioning, even though such vital questions as the death of her husband and the death of her father

were used. At one point I told her that her mother had died (which was false) to closely observe her emotional response and still there was none. During this entire time, it was quite obvious that she was and has been grasping her left breast with her left hand for a long time.[159]

This report also gave an account of McCollum's paranoia, which caused her to suspect "imaginary gases or poisons" and that "people [were] trying to poison her with her food."

Evans faults the court-appointed psychiatrists for not citing the stress resulting from Adams's abuse, or the stress of her prison abortion, as contributing factors in her mental status at the time of the second trial.[160]

But what Evans fails to acknowledge is that the court-ordered psychiatric examination of McCollum before her trial was for the purpose of determining her ability to rationally participate in her own defense and was necessarily limited to that question alone. The purpose was not to explore the etiology of any mental illness, or its specific nature, beyond assessing whether her mental state rendered her unable to proceed with her defense at her trial.

In keeping with the stated purpose of the court-ordered psychiatric interview—to determine McCollum's ability to participate rationally in her own defense—the psychiatrist concludes, "It is my opinion that this patient is delusional…" and "for these reasons, I believe that she is unable to carry on a rational defense due to her present mental condition, which is definitely abnormal." The final recommendation is that, "she should be committed to a psychiatric hospital for observation and treatment of her mental illness until she is well."

By today's standards, the examination was unethical, since no psychotherapist today would tell a disturbed patient that her mother had died when she had not, just to elicit a response. But at the time, there were no such standards, so the psychiatrist cannot be faulted for a breach of professional ethics that did not yet exist.

Judge Adams also ordered two other psychiatrists, Drs. McCullagh and Ingram, both from Jacksonville, to evaluate McCollum. Their examination was far more detailed than Dr. Moore's. It included interviews with Matt McCollum, Ruby's brother, and the jailers, Mr. and Mrs. Cannon, who reported that she had frequent crying spells. More importantly, Ruby McCollum, after asking that the jailers leave the cell, spoke to Dr. McCullagh about her belief that she was being poisoned, and pleaded, "Doctor, get me out of here." Although she spoke in short sentences, she was nonetheless responsive to his questions and complied with his physical examination.[161]

Drs. McCullagh and Ingram wrote a letter to the court that was decisive, stating that McCollum was "psychotic (insane), suffering from a prison psychosis." The letter went on to state that "due to this mental condition, it is our opinion that she is not in condition to conduct a rational defense."[162]

At the hearing on September 24, 1954, William Slaughter, the state's attorney, asked, "Doctor, does that mean she's crazy?" McCullagh replied that "she is now suffering from a 'situation crisis' or 'prison psychosis,' and by this we mean mental illness."[163]

This 1950s analysis of McCollum's psychotic break, based on symptoms described by her physicians at the time, is certainly more medically accurate than Evans's proposition involving the "colonizing" of African women in the early 1800s to explain McCollum's symptoms.

What is known about Ruby McCollum's deportment during her sanity hearing of September 24, 1954, only days after the psychiatric examination declaring her unfit to stand trial, comes from Huie's observations:

> There, for the first time, I saw Ruby. She sat with McGriff on the defense side of the table. I nodded as McGriff told her who I was. I had received many letters from her; and now, to spite Cannon, she credited me with getting the new trial. She tried to taunt him by saying that he "hadn't done nothing" for her but take her money, and that I was her only friend.[164]

It is noteworthy that Huie saw McGriff speaking with McCollum after she had been determined to be completely uncommunicative only days earlier.[165]

It is also noteworthy that she seemed to believe that Huie, rather than her actual attorney, Frank Cannon, had come to represent her. Whether this belief was related to the "Hon." title that Huie gave himself in the earlier proposed power of attorney is unknown.

Also, as mentioned earlier, the jailers, Mr. and Mrs. Cannon (no relation to her attorney), insisted to Dr. McCullagh, during his psychiatric examination, that McCollum was sane. They said, for example, that she could remember the long address of her son, Sam Jr., who was stationed in the Army. They also maintained that she had just written him before her psychiatric examination.[166]

These behaviors indicate, at least at some level, that Ruby McCollum could function during the month. Also, for the weeks before the murder, it is difficult if not impossible to separate Ruby McCollum's physical complaints from her mental condition. Aside from many psychosomatic illnesses, there are also many conditions, known in medical literature as "masquerades," in which the signs, symptoms, and patterns of medical diseases can present as psychological problems. Masquerades defy the dualistic categorization of diseases as being either physical or mental, with no exploration of interactions between the two to arrive at the true etiology of the condition.[167]

Such medical distinctions were not commonly understood in 1952, and there is insufficient historical evidence to pursue the topic.

Confirmation Bias and McCollum's Medications

Researchers and producers of documentaries ensnare themselves in another confirmation bias by accepting as gospel the very specific list of medications that Ruby details in her letters, and which, she maintains, Adams used to control her.[168]

She also mentions a specific medication, alleging that personnel at Raiford used it to make her sneeze and be unable to sleep at night.[169] To date, no one has researched this list to refute or substantiate McCollum's allegations.

McCollum's list of medications, as she spelled and capitalized them, includes the following:

1. Protolac
2. Viasineral
3. Manganease Permangunate
4. Thiamine
5. Procaine Penicillin
6. Thiamine Hydrochloride
7. Cinagil
8. Panthodrene
9. Phenocin
10. Pento Extract
11. Ioda Lake-S
12. Hystadil

Vi-syneral (McCollum's "Viasineral"), manganese permanganate, thiamine, and thiamine hydrochloride are vitamins and minerals. Procaine penicillin is a form of the antibiotic. None of these are poisonous, although individual adverse effects cannot be ruled out.

The remaining eight medications do not appear in the 1950 edition of *The Merck Manual*. Indeed, the manual lists only forty-four prescription medications used in the profession at the time.

A search of the 1937 publication *Toxicology*—available to Adams when he was in pharmacy school before attending medical school—also yielded no results.

After searching several pharmacological databases, the author enlisted the resources of the Arizona Poison and Drug Information Center, whose director, Keith Boesen, PharmD, CSPI, replied:

We searched much of the Internet and several pharmacy-related databases we could think of. We even searched an old card catalog database that was created in the '50s and '60s by the founder of our poison center, Dr. Albert Picchioni.[170]

Dr. Boesen found only the following two medications listed by McCollum:

1. Hystadil

   Histadil (Histadyl) is an antihistamine that is used primarily in the treatment of allergic reactions.

   WITH THERAPEUTIC USE

   ADVERSE EFFECTS: COMMON: Mild sedation, dizziness, impaired coordination, and mild anticholinergic effects. Paradoxical excitation can develop in some patients.

   WITH POISONING/EXPOSURE

   MILD TO MODERATE POISONING: Somnolence, anticholinergic effects (i.e., mydriasis, flushing, fever, dry mouth, and decreased bowel sounds), tachycardia, mild hypertension, and nausea and vomiting are common after overdose. Agitation, confusion, and hallucinations may develop with moderate poisoning.
   SEVERE POISONING: Severe effects may include agitated delirium, psychosis, seizures, coma, hypotension, QRS widening, and ventricular dysrhythmias, including torsade de pointe but are generally only reported in adults after very large, deliberate ingestions. Rhabdomyolysis and renal failure may rarely develop in patients with prolonged agitation, coma, or seizures.

2. Phenonian

   According to the Poison Control Center, Phenocin and or Phenonian (fenocin) is a penicillin drug used to treat bacterial infections. McCollum reported having frequent injections of Penicillin.

WITH THERAPEUTIC USE

ADVERSE EFFECTS: COMMON: GASTROINTESTINAL: Nausea, vomiting, diarrhea, epigastric distress, and black hairy tongue are likely with orally administered penicillins. RENAL: Renal failure, crystalluria, interstitial nephritis, and hemorrhagic cystitis have been reported following the use of penicillin derivatives. Symptoms are frequently associated with sensitivity reactions and may include the following: DERMATOLOGY: Dermatologic reactions can vary greatly in severity, character, and distribution. Amoxicillin and ampicillin appears to cause skin rashes more frequently than other penicillins. HEMATOLOGIC: Thrombocytopenia, neutropenia, and agranulocytosis have occurred following administration of the semisynthetic penicillins and may be related to a hypersensitivity reaction.

WITH POISONING/EXPOSURE

MILD TO MODERATE TOXICITY: Nausea, vomiting, abdominal pain and diarrhea may develop with ingestion. Skin rashes and urticaria may develop, especially with amoxicillin and ampicillin ingestions. Hematuria, crystalluria and transient renal insufficiency have been reported after amoxicillin overdose.

SEVERE TOXICITY: Agitation, confusion, hallucinations, stupor, coma, multifocal myoclonus, seizures and encephalopathy may occur following massive doses of IV penicillins (40 to 100 million units/day). Cardiac arrest and death have been associated with inadvertent intravenous administration of penicillin G (benzathine and procaine). Hyperkalemia may also develop.

Penicillins Poisindex. 2015 Truven Health Analytics Inc. MICROMEDEX(R) Healthcare Series Vol. 163 expires 3/2015

Neither of the above medications reported by McCollum would have been poisonous if given at a therapeutic dose. As with most medications, an overdose of any of them would produce the noted side effects.

As mentioned earlier, McCollum reported that when she was given Phenocin at Raiford, she sneezed and could not sleep at night, but these symptoms are not associated adverse effects of this medication.

This leaves the following five medications that McCollum reported receiving but that could not be identified in any medical manual of the period or through extensive research at the poison control center:

1. Protolac
2. Cinagil
3. Panthodrene
4. Pento Extract
5. Ioda Lake-S

Protolac and the vitamin Vi-syneral were the combination of medications that McCollum mentions Adams giving her, stating that it would make her "crazy as hell in a few months."[171]

In the same letter, McCollum maintains that Protolac "destroyes [destroys] the organs, makes one ache in the joints give one pneumonia or TB's [TB] if it isn't taken out of ones body."

This combination of adverse symptoms due to toxicology is not to be found in medical literature.

Another approach to considering the alleged side effects of drugs administered to McCollum is to read what she said about *why* they were given to her. The following three statements, in her first letters from the Suwannee County Jail, speak to the point:

> When he get mad at me he would tare [tear] into me like a lion. Plus give me a big shot of medicine to almost kill me.
>
> I ask why would you want to do [me] that way? He said it takes a little of that for you some times.
>
> I thought of some medicine he had given me. It was two CC of Ioda lake-S that was the only thing eased my head and heart. But I continued to feal [feel] foolish in my head. And hurt in my joints. He gave me these shots because I told him if he would give me something to get it out I wouldn't ever ask him to do anything else for me.

(The above statements appear in Appendix B as, "Second Set of Pages.")

It is apparent that Adams gave her injections of *something* to control her behavior. But an exhaustive search reveals that neither Protolac, the alleged poison, nor Ioda lake-S, the alleged antidote, appears anywhere in medical literature or in any major toxicological archive of the era.

This kind of magical thinking, by which one can "drink this" and fall deadly ill, and then "drink that" and be perfectly well again, is reminiscent of *Alice's Adventures in Wonderland.*

Another consideration that researchers of this story seem never to have entertained is the possibility of a negative placebo, or "nocebo," effect—itself a form of magical thinking.

In 1961, Walter Kennedy coined the term "nocebo," Latin for "I will harm," as the counterpart of "placebo" (I will please).[172] The term came into usage a few years after Henry Beecher published his seminal paper on the placebo effect.[173]

The nocebo effect occurs after administering an inert drug, and the responses generated are due entirely to the subject's pessimistic belief and expectation that the inert drug in question will produce harmful, unpleasant, or undesirable consequences.

Given McCollum's susceptibility to vague aches and pains and her constantly seeking what she believed to be quick fixes through vitamin B12 and penicillin injections, it is even more likely that she would be susceptible to the nocebo effect.[174]

Since Adams was a sociopath and was known to abuse women (as reported not only by McCollum but also by others, including Edith Park, his nurse anesthetist), it is possible that he injected McCollum with a perfectly harmless placebo, such as an isotonic saline solution, while telling her that it was a poison. Then, when she had undergone sufficient mental anguish to knuckle under and do what he told her, he would give her the "antidote."

Using the nocebo effect to control McCollum rather than actually injecting her with harmful drugs is in keeping with his refusal (mentioned in the same letter cited above) to give her a tubal ligation, telling her, "Lot of women wish they had the healthy ovaries or organs you have."

After all, if he refused to disable her "healthy ovaries" with surgery, why would he destroy them with poison?

It is also more credible that the nocebo effect was in play than that McCollum was injected with injurious drugs, not only by Adams, but also by medical personnel at Brewster Hospital, Raiford State Prison, and the Suwannee County Jail.

Confirmation Bias and McCollum's Understanding of Her Trial

In Lesson 2 of a classroom study guide designed as a companion piece for the documentary *You Belong to Me,* author Ruth Thompson-Miller asks her students, "Did Ruby McCollum understand what was going on in the courtroom?"[175]

Aside from a brief history of Jim Crow in Lesson 1, students are given no information from which they can arrive at an informed response to this question.

What the students do not have is a copy of the following two excerpts from Ruby McCollum's letters to her attorneys, written in the Suwannee County Jail:

> Continue to use the defence [defense] relationship—six yrs. He is the father of my baby. He let my husband run nos. for my sake. He wanted me to get on the table Aug 3.[176]
> ------------------------------

Mr. Cogdill was over here Thursday evening ask when had I saw you I said Monday. He said he talked to you Wednesday night & yesterday morning. Then he said he wanted to get my people together if I would give him a note to give Buck. He wants the rest of his money if he can get it. I told him Buck wasn't going to pay him all of it now no way. He said you know I can have this thing set up or reversed. I didn't say anything. He also something about a phyciatrist [psychiatrist]. Then he wanted to know if I got along as good here as did in Raiford. I said I don't know.[177]

Here, as elsewhere in her letters, Ruby McCollum demonstrates that she not only understands the details of her trial but also is in control, directing her defense, coordinating with her brother-in-law to retain legal representation to advance her trial, and deciding which documents she would or would not sign. (Ruby McCollum's letters are reproduced in Appendix B.)

In the documentary *You Belong to Me*, Tammy Evans appears to question the legal definition of "insanity," which would also imply that Ruby McCollum did not understand what she did when she murdered Adams: "I think a really good question to ask is how you define sanity. What Ruby did was perhaps challenging the definition of what sanity and insanity meant."[178]

Perhaps the best response to Evans's question is the definition of "sanity," for purposes of the law, found in *West's Encyclopedia of American Law:* "reasonable understanding; sound mind; possessing mental faculties that are capable of distinguishing right from wrong so as to bear legal responsibility for one's actions."[179]

Figure 11: View from judge's bench showing main entrance and flanking staircases leading to "Colored" balconies.

Figure 12: View from courtroom entrance.

Confirmation Bias and Ruby McCollum's Innocence

Not a shred of evidence supports claims that Ruby McCollum was innocent of Adams's murder. And yet, former Live Oak city councilman, Doug Udell, openly admits in his interview in "The Shot Doctor": "My daddy told me not to get too close to no white person." He also states, "I haven't found *one* black person in Suwannee County who believes she did it, and never *did* believe it."[180]

Ironically, Mr. Udell's father, who gave him this advice, was a white man.

Mr. Udell is apparently unaware of the many interviews with African American residents of Live Oak that reporters from the *Pittsburgh Courier* conducted right after the murder.

"The Shot Doctor" also supports the conjecture that people in Live Oak held this opinion. It does so by having its narrator state the outright lie that Ruby McCollum did not testify at her own trial.

Since Ruby McCollum herself, along with two other African American witnesses, testified during her trial that she did indeed commit the murder, suggesting that someone else pulled the trigger is confirmation bias at its worst.

Even Ruby McCollum's own sister, Mrs. Lillian Shuman, states in her interview for *You Belong to Me*, "She messed up a good thing. If she hadn't let down her family, she would not have been in that serious trouble."[181]

Then there are Ruby McCollum's own words, also reported by her sister in the same film, when the sister and their mother, Gertrude, went to visit Ruby in the Suwannee County Jail: "We went up there to see her and my mama asked, 'Why'd you have to kill the doc for?' She said, ''Cause I want to.'"

There is perhaps no better witness to Ruby McCollum's guilt than her own sister.

Confirmation Bias and the Ethics of A. K. Black, State's Attorney

In *You Belong to Me,* a voiceover quotes Zora Hurston relating that Arthur Keith Black, the prosecuting attorney during the McCollum trial, left his office to represent Adams's widow, Mrs. Florrie Lee Adams, in her wrongful-death lawsuit against Ruby McCollum's portion of the estate.

Immediately following the voiceover, Mrs. Edna R. Hindson, A. K. Black's daughter, says this:

> Dad *did* want to watch out for her [Mrs. Adams]. He was like that. He had
> a big heart. Yes he could be very, very firm, but he had a big heart for people

that he thought were not being treated fairly . . . you know . . . under the circumstance that . . . you know . . . their husband being murdered.[182]

By today's standards, an attorney does not fight for the conviction of a defendant in a murder trial and then take the lead in filing a wrongful-death suit for the widow of the victim. The conflict of interest is obvious.

That aside, Black did not resign in order to take on the wrongful-death lawsuit out of compassion or any other sentiment toward Mrs. Adams. In fact, the following chain of events led to his leaving the office of state's attorney:

1. On May 8, 1952, Black learned that he had lost his reelection bid as state's attorney in the seven-county Third Judicial Circuit, to Randolph Slaughter by a vote of 12,250 to 9,236.[183] Black's term was thus slated to end on December 31, 1952.

2. According to a letter from the Florida Comptroller's Office, on October 16, 1952 (reproduced on next page), Black filed an application with the director of the Florida Retirement System in the Comptroller's Office, for total and permanent disability.[184]

3. According to the same letter, from November 14, 1952, until November 20, 1952, Black was examined by a physician and declared to be "totally and permanently disabled from performing the work required of him as State Attorney, Third Judicial Circuit."

4. On December 17, 1952, jurors were sworn in for the trial of Ruby McCollum, and Black, who had been declared fully and permanently disabled at the time, continued in his position as state's attorney in the prosecution of Ruby McCollum.

5. On December 20, 1952, the jury returned the verdict of "guilty of first-degree murder" for Ruby McCollum.

6. On December 24, 1952, Black retired under the Retirement System's disability clause. According to the letter from the Florida Comptroller's Office, "Mr. Black was paid benefits from December 24 due to the fact that he did not resign as State Attorney until December 23, 1952."

To say that Black "retired" for any reason after losing the election is inaccurate since he had no choice but to leave the office at the end of his elected term.

Instead, it is apparent that Black secured Ruby McCollum's conviction before "retiring" on full disability from the State of Florida after he lost his reelection bid as state's attorney and before his term of office expired. It is also apparent that he did not leave his office out of the goodness of his heart so that he might take on the case of Adams's widow in her wrongful-death suit.

Huie had evidently asked the Comptroller's Office whether Black could continue his prosecution of McCollum after he was determined to be "totally and permanently disabled," to which Ms. Mawhinney, the director of the Retirement System, replied, "It has never been tested in the Courts of the State whether after a person retires under disability, he can continue to follow his profession or work in some limited capacity."

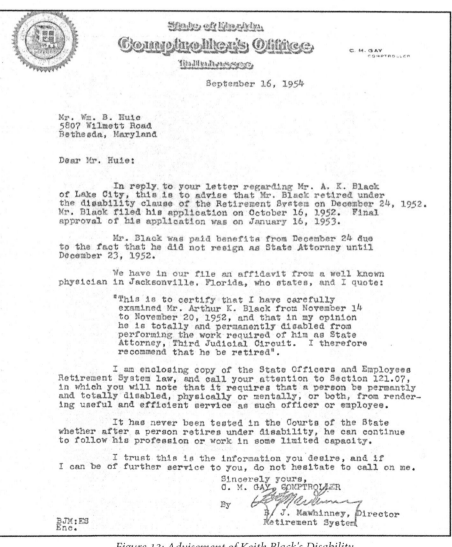

Figure 13: Advisement of Keith Black's Disability.

By today's standards, filing for total and permanent disability while continuing to work would be considered insurance fraud.

In 1977, Black was indicted by a federal grand jury on charges of conspiracy to obstruct justice in connection with alleged racketeering in the Live Oak-Lake City area.[185] Huie had alleged Black's involvement in bolita during his contempt hearing many years earlier.

Charges were later dropped after Black suffered a severe heart attack in a time when coronary artery bypasses were relatively new and heart attacks were usually extremely debilitating or fatal.

Confirmation Bias and Ruby McCollum's Place of Burial

In the photographs below, which I took, Ruby McCollum's grave is on the left, and Matt Jackson's grave is on the right, behind the Hopewell Baptist Church, just north of Live Oak, Florida.

Figure 14: Ruby McCollum's Grave, Hopewell Baptist Church North of Live Oak, Florida

One of the conspiracy theories surrounding the authenticity of Ruby McCollum's place of burial concerns the fact that her death certificate contains two errors: her surname is misspelled "McCollumn," and her burial location is listed as a "rural cemetery near Ocala, Florida."

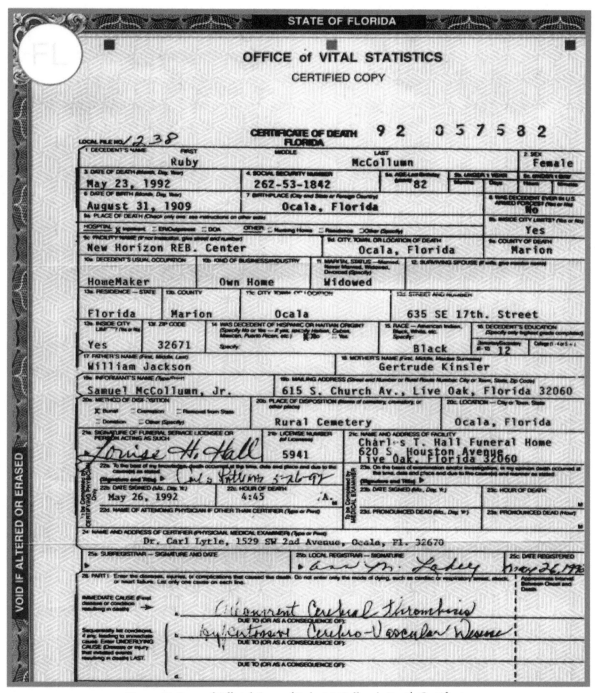

Figure 15: Copy of Official Copy of Ruby McCollum's Death Certificate.

Anyone familiar with the McCollum name in Live Oak is aware that "McCollumn" was a common spelling variant, along with "McCollom" and McCullum." Indeed, Zora Hurston, in a letter to Huie dated July 28, 1954, spells it "McCollom."[186] Also, the first article on the trial, by John A. Diaz in the August 16, 1952, *Pittsburgh Courier,* spells the name "McCullum."[187]

Aside from these errors, McCollum's undertaker and her physician signed the certificate, and the place, cause, and date of death are all correct.

Conspiracy theorists should consider that a death certificate is required to be filled out by a funeral director and appropriately signed and filed with the local registrar for the State, *before* a funeral. Should the family change its decision about burial or cremation arrangements, including the cemetery where their loved one is to be interred, there is no law requiring a change to the death certificate for it to remain a legal document.

But conspiracy theorists maintain that Ruby McCollum was more likely interred in the Jackson family cemetery in Zuber, Florida (the "rural cemetery near Ocala" mentioned on the death certificate), in an attempt to hide the whereabouts of her remains. The Union Cemetery, where many of her relatives are interred, would be a poor choice by anyone wishing to hide her burial site. While it is off of paved roads, anyone with a county map can easily find it.

The entrance to the Union Cemetery, shown on the next page, has a cattle gate, which was unlocked when I went there. While many of Ruby McCollum's family members are buried there—including Bessie and Walter Jackson, whose headstones are shown below—no marker commemorates Ruby McCollum. To believe that she would be buried in a family plot with no marker stretches the imagination and journeys into the netherworld of "facts" that cannot be disproved.

The family evidently first decided that this remote rural cemetery north of Live Oak was a safer place to bury Matt Jackson, even though he died many years after the murder. Otherwise, the logical choice would have been to bury him beside his wife, Bessie, and many of his brothers and sisters, in the Jackson family cemetery in Zuber.

Reliable evidence of Ruby McCollum's burial site is in the testimony of her undertaker and family business partner, Charles Hall, who was interviewed by the former Florida film commissioner, Ms. Jude Hagin. In an e-mail received December 21, 2014, Ms. Hagin states:

> I interviewed Charles Hall in April of 2002. Towards the end of our long interview, I asked if he handled Ruby's funeral when she died and he said he did. He told me where she was buried, and I told him I already had been to her grave to pay my respects. I asked who put her grave marker there and he told me that he did. He took me into the "chapel" where they held services and told me about Ruby's funeral.[188]

Ms. Hagin has interviewed many McCollum family members and friends who attended the funeral, and she agrees that Ruby McCollum is interred at her marked grave in the cemetery of the Hopewell Baptist Church.

Despite my sharing all the foregoing information with Evans, she chose to question the legality of the death certificate, relying instead on the word of a local Zuber undertaker that the death certificate could not be valid, since "such a vague listing, he said, was not permitted under state guidelines."[189]

It is troubling that Evans would cite a misspelled surname and a local undertaker's opinion on a vaguely stated place of burial as proof that the death certificate is not a legal document. It is particularly concerning that she published this statement in her book without contacting the Florida Bureau of Vital Statistics, in Jacksonville, to get its official explanation.

When I did just that, I received this reply (emphasis added):

> This office may amend the death record (05/23/1992) based upon an affidavit signed by the listed informant on the death record or by the next of kin. **These would be minor corrections. The death record as filed is a legal document.** Florida Statute allows this office, which maintains vital records, the authority to correct any misstatement, error or omission which may occur on the record.[190]

The e-mail is signed by Ms. Betty Shannon, program administrator of the Records Amendment Section of the Florida Bureau of Vital Statistics, who based her determination on chapter 382 of Florida Statutes, which specifies the information that must be contained in a legally filed death certificate.

Instead of looking for the facts, as I did, Evans dedicates five pages of her book to her ordeal in searching out what she characterizes as a practically impossible place to find.

I, on the other hand, found the Union Cemetery quite easily and took the photographs on the following page.

Evans recounts her visit to the Jackson family graveyard: "There lay Sonja's grave, marked only with a tin plate that bore her name and her birth and death dates. And directly next to Sonja was a gentle swell in the grassy earth that could very well be Ruby McCollum's unmarked final resting place."[191]

I suppose it did not occur to Evans that the dirt remaining after excavation for Sonja's burial might have been left on an empty plot next to the grave, resulting in just such a "gentle swell in the grassy earth." Indeed, if she had bothered to look around, she would have found many such gentle swells throughout the cemetery.

Evans concludes that "even though I have no proof of this supposition . . . I somehow sense that she *is* there."[192]

Then Evans's confirmation bias becomes blatantly obvious when she describes her feelings at the imagined gravesite of Ruby McCollum:

> Or perhaps it is because I have become so acutely aware of the silence and secrecy that enveloped McCollum during her lifetime that I cannot imagine her without them even in death . . . There, for the first time since my immersion in this project, I heard echoes of redemption in what until then had been only endless southern silences filled with suffering.[193]

Here, in Evans's epiphany, she resorts, not to archival evidence and state authority, but to a final conspiracy theory to support her thesis of "silence and secrecy" in the McCollum case.

A final touch of irony is that Evans uses the picture of the headstone from Ruby McCollum's *actual* place of burial north of Live Oak on her book's back cover, suggesting that she would have the story both ways.

Figure 1: Zuber, Florida Cemetery. Burial Site of Ruby McCollum's Relatives.

CHAPTER 4:
AN ALTERNATIVE TO CONFIRMATION
AND PRESENTIST BIASES

The story of Ruby McCollum embodies a moral dilemma: What should a black woman in the Jim Crow South do to terminate an unwanted pregnancy and get out of an abusive affair with a white man when she has no recourse in the law? Should she move out of town and have an illegal abortion, or stay and kill her lover?

Readers of the *Pittsburgh Courier* were given the chance to offer their opinions on Ruby McCollum's actions after Zora Hurston's last installment of "The Life Story of Mrs. Ruby J. McCollum!" ended abruptly with the May 2, 1953 issue. That issue announced the next installment, which never appeared.

Instead, the May 9 issue replaced Hurston's series with the column "Ruby! Good or Bad?" Comments from readers poured in. Some were sure she had been framed for the murder; others laid the blame squarely on her shoulders. Some applauded her courage in standing up to a white man, while others condemned her for violating one of the Ten Commandments.

The question of Ruby McCollum's guilt is a valid one, so I presented it to a friend who is a Catholic priest, adding that he was to assume that McCollum did not fire in self-defense. His answer was that murder is a cardinal sin, whereas abuse is not, so leaving town, rather than killing her abuser, would have been the morally right thing to do. He added, of course, that any choice to have an abortion would also be a mortal sin.

Clearly, today, the nature of the moral dilemma would be entirely different. Ruby McCollum could obtain a restraining order against Adams and try to reconcile with her husband. After all, it is doubtful that a man with Adams's political ambitions would defy such an order today. Regarding the choice whether to have an abortion, the turmoil over her moral dilemma would depend on the strength of her beliefs as a fundamentalist Christian.

But that is today, and Ruby McCollum lived in the 1950s, when black people left town if they found themselves at odds with a white person—especially one in a position of power.

A clear example of this was when the McCollums' predecessor, bolita king L. J. Hopps, fled town after being threatened by the same men who drowned his student for daring to send a Christmas card with an admittedly romantic sentiment to a white female coworker at Van Priest's five-and-ten.

But Ruby McCollum chose differently. Against overwhelming odds, according to her own African American attorney, Releford McGriff, she chose to plan a murder and construct a scenario of self-defense.

In her own words, McCollum said of the murder, "I don't know whether I did right or whether I did wrong." She also confided in her sister, who, visiting her in the Suwannee County Jail, asked the simple question "Why?" The answer: "Because I want[ed] to."

Viewed in this light, and listening to her own words, Ruby McCollum knew that her choice did not fit neatly into the societally constructed categories of right and wrong. Instead, her choice to murder Adams was an *amoral* choice—outside the cultural boundaries established by both religion and the law.

A totally different approach to understanding the story of Ruby McCollum would be to step outside time, into a sort of existentialist twilight zone devoid of Judeo-Christian morality and devoid of statutory or common law. In this construct, the question of Ruby McCollum's guilt or innocence becomes not whether she broke the law when she shot Adams, and not whether she did "right" or "wrong." The question becomes whether she acted *authentically* when she pulled the trigger.

To this point, Evans writes [emphasis added]:

> There is no denying that McCollum broke the law that Sunday morning she murdered Adams, but she did not act without a sense of justice; it was justice **by her own definition.** And if she was not physically in church that day, I am convinced that when she methodically pulled the trigger she looked—**on her own terms**—full on the face of God.[194]

Evans's conviction that McCollum acted "on her own terms," and "by her own definition" parallels Hurston's reporting on the trial, during a point when McCollum is on the stand, testifying about the murder (emphasis added):

> What I beheld in the eyes of Ruby McCollum in that instant when she balked into silence, when the agony of her memories robbed her of the power of speech for a time, may God be kind and never permit me to behold again. In a flash, I comprehended the **spatial infinity of the human mind, that mother of monsters and angels, and the ineffable glory and unspeakable horror of its creations.**[195]

Hurston, who was present at the trial, had a chance to look on Ruby McCollum's face as she testified to killing Adams. It was in that moment that Hurston sensed something transcendent as McCollum appeared to face the creation of her own mind.

Later, at her sentencing, Hurston observed McCollum and wrote:

> The discerning spectator could not avoid the conclusion that here was no ordinary mortal, no cringing victim inadequate in its fate. There sat an extraordinary personality. Here was a woman, a Negro woman, with the courage to date every fate, to boldly attack every tradition of her surroundings and even the age-old laws of every land.[196]

All the evidence indicates that killing Adams was a reasoned choice and a very personal act for Ruby McCollum. It occurred on his turf and at close range. Even the handgun used by McCollum was an "up close and personal" weapon, a .32-caliber nickel-plated Smith and Wesson revolver, manufactured about 1915 and given to her by her husband to defend herself while he was away on frequent business trips to Tampa.[197] This handgun was originally marketed as a "gentleman's card table" or "vest" weapon and later became known as a "belly gun," designed to be easily concealed and used at point-blank range—which is exactly how Ruby McCollum used it to shoot Adams.

The murder was well planned, and designed to appear as an act of self-defense, as seen in McCollum's letter to her attorney from the Suwannee County Jail, instructing him on how to conduct her defense.

There is every indication that Ruby McCollum decided to take control of the relationship—and possibly even of the trial's outcome.

Some would call this mind-set insane. Others, looking back with an existentialist eye to evaluate her decision outside the confines of the race, class, and gender restrictions of the Jim Crow South, might call it "authentic."

"Authenticity" is a technical term used in varying versions of existentialism to explain the degree to which one is true to one's own personality or character, despite external pressures of society, culture, and the law. The "conscious self" is seen as coming to terms with being in a material world and with encountering external forces, pressures, and influences that are very different from, and "other than" itself.

In an existentialist context, a lack of authenticity is considered bad faith. Viewed in these terms, the decision to perform an authentic act resides solely within the individual.

Frederick Douglass was such a man in the Antebellum South where he was considered chattel because of his race. He was a white man's property like his horse or his cow. Douglass chose to defy both his master and the laws of the land to gain his freedom. Once he had claimed his freedom, he became a great orator, author and social activist confidant of President Abraham Lincoln. When the Civil War ended, he became the U. S. Ambassador to Haiti.

While Ruby McCollum never rose to the ranks of a Frederick Douglass, she was also an authentic person who created her own values to bring meaning to her life through a steadfast commitment to define herself according to her own terms, regardless of the race, class, and gender issues that she faced in the Jim Crow South.

In doing so and demanding to speak in her own defense at her trial, she set a legal precedent for an African American woman testifying to being abused and forced to bear a white man's child.

And so, as is often the case, social justice progresses one painful step at a time.

AFTERWORD

On a very personal note, I am saddened by the recent revisionist takes on Ruby McCollum's story mentioned in this work, primarily because they squander talent and resources that could otherwise be invested in more important projects.

Every day, twenty years after I supposedly retired, I work alongside my psychologist wife and hear the gut-wrenching stories of poorly educated, lower-income women, along with their children, who are abused by their husbands.

From time to time, I will sit with these abused women as I assist with the psychometrics of their case, record their histories, and reflect some variant of the following:

> Ms. Jones, I see that you have had three previous boyfriends and have had a child with each of them. Now you are beginning a relationship with a fourth man, and you are pregnant after living together for several months. I also see that you say that this man you are living with is the love of your life, whereas all the other three are demons straight from hell who pounded you senseless. Is it possible that in the beginning of each relationship you felt the same about each of those three as you do about your current boyfriend?

Inevitably, I get the same wide-eyed look and surprised response: "How did you know?"

Since I am not a counselor, all I can tell them is that my wife, the psychologist, will refer them for DBT training. What I cannot tell them is that they will very likely be diagnosed with borderline personality disorder, which is often caused by early physical and or sexual abuse, abandonment, or other childhood trauma, and is frequently associated with a resulting fear of abandonment and unstable relationships.

All this causes me to lament that the women my wife and I work with rarely read, so they would not benefit by being referred to the many books on the subject.

These women do, however, watch television and would greatly benefit from a documentary or training film on the "red flags" of abusive relationships, and how to spot the kind of man they should avoid.

But no such films are available.

Then I get more than a little frustrated that so much time and money has been spent by feminist filmmakers visiting and revisiting Ruby McCollum's story, which happened to a single woman over half a century ago, when they could be out there making a very real difference in the lives of hundreds of thousands of women and children today.

ACKNOWLEDGEMENTS

First, my wife, the psychologist, is owed a deeply felt vote of gratitude for teaching me the psychological dynamics at play between Ruby McCollum and Dr. C. LeRoy Adams, Jr.

While I can no longer speak with him since he has moved on to a higher plane, I owe a huge thanks to my father, who talked with me for hours at a time about this story, and shared his conversations with Dr. Adams and others who worked with him at the Suwannee County Hospital.

While my mother was less open about this story, she also shared insights into the longsuffering Mrs. C. LeRoy Adams, Jr. (Florrie Lee Adams) who was her friend. Mrs. Adams's plight was typical of the wife of a politically powerful man of the time in that she had little identity of her own.

A special thanks to Keith Boesen, PharmD, CSPI, director of the Arizona Poison and Drug Information Center, for enlisting his graduate students to assist him in conducting a thorough search of the literature regarding Ruby McCollum's self-reported list of medications.

The staff at the Thompson Library at the Ohio State University in Columbus, Ohio was extremely helpful in assisting me in my research on the William Huie Papers there, and in furnishing copies of materials used in this work. The staff at the Smathers Library at the University of Florida in Gainesville, Florida was also extremely helpful in assisting me with examining the letters of Zora Neale Hurston.

Eric Musgrove in the Clerk of the Court office at the Suwannee County Courthouse has proven to be a great source regarding the historical aspects of this trial, and his friendship, time and assistance are appreciated.

Carl McCurdy, M.D., my personal physician, loaned me the antiquarian medical books cited in this work. I could not rest easy until I had returned these cherished tomes.

I owe Jude Hagin, my pen pal on the Ruby McCollum story over the years, thanks for her verification of Ruby McCollum's place and manner of burial. I also applaud her documentary, *You Belong to Me*, even though I differ with some of its tenets. That said, archiving the opinions and observations of Live Oak residents and Adams and McCollum relatives plays an important role in this story from a sociological standpoint, and creates a launching pad for continued debate.

There are hundreds of readers of my previous works on this story who have written to me, asking to remain anonymous, who have furnished additional insights into this story, including a love child of Dr. Adams by a white paramour, a cell mate of Ruby McCollum, and several McCollum "writers" in their bolita business. Their insights have contributed immensely to this work.

Finally, my long-suffering and very patient editor, Michael J. Carr, is appreciated for his ability to polish my manuscript for the first edition of this work.

ACKNOWLEDGMENTS

APPENDIX A:
EDITH PARK NOTES AND LETTERS

c/o Lister Hill Hospital,
1315 South Military St.,
Hamilton, Alabama,
March 10th, 1954.

William Bradford Huie,
Garden City, Alabama.

Dear Mr. Huie:

Forgive the delay; but in moving, I didn't have hardly the
time to write home, let alone do business correspondence.

As you probably discovered, upon your arrival in Chicago,
I started working here, March 1st. I would like to have been able
to have seen you in Chicago. However, perhaps it can be arranged
here somehow, on one of my week-ends off. I am off every-other-
week-end, starting this week-end, the 13th.

I don't suppose there is much that I can help you with,
Dr. Adams was just a general run-of-the-mill genius.

Will be glad to hear from you.

Sincerely,

Edith M. Park, R.N

Edith Marion Park, R.N.

Only a brief note to say: Look up a Mr. Colin Barnes - either an alcoholic, or had been given enough dope, then taken off it, that maybe money was easily obtained from him, then. He used to go with a Mrs. Bevan - widow - a pretty dark-haird woman. He disgraced his whole family; his daughter pretty much ran all his affairs, including his farm, and lumber, I think. I think the disgrace-part was pretty much handled by Dr. A. He built it up to look much worse than it was. For some reason. Brody Harris and I, at Dr. Adams order slipped him off to Jax in the dead of the night - so no one would know - to an "alcoholic" home there. Dr. Adams said, "Give him only barbiturates". But, they didn't hold him, and I slipped him 200 mgm. (4 cc., I believe) of Demerol on the way, and he started acting normal. So, I knew then that he was on Demerol, and Dr. Adams was making it look like alcohol

Note above and note below were on same sheet of paper, but re-inserted in typewriter so that each was upside down relative to one another.

Mail all your correspondence to me in a PLAIN envelope too. Those postal people in Live Oak don't miss anything. They'd wonder why I would be getting mail from YOU!!!

Ansell Brown: name of one funeral director. The decent one, I think.
Dewey North "bought" an adopted baby from Dr. Adams. Dr. Adams "sold" many illegitimate babies around to people that wanted children and couldn't have them. But, I imagine some paid through the nose. Of course the baby's mothers never got a dime.

Friday P.M.,
                                        Here.

Dear Bill:

     Oh! How sweet can people be! What did you do
that for! It was a wonderful surprise and, a wonderful Easter gift. What a big bonnet you must expect me to buy, with $50.00. I thank you ever so
much, and will show you what I mean when I next
see you!Which will be, May 7th in Jacksonville.

     What a fiasco to-day has been!! A character
many times worse than Dr. Adams ever hoped to be,
lives right here in Hamilton. Want, that I should
collect some material on him, while I'm here? His
name is Dr. J.O. Brooks; heavy drug-addict; perhaps a mainliner. A thorough disgrace to the Medical profession!! And that is putting mildly - a
vast understatement!!!!!!!!!!!!!!!!!!!!!!!!!!!!!!!!!!!

     He came home one night from being "drunk" on
narcotics, and beat their little girl up, and the
wife shot him, and missed; hit him in the thigh. He
is in it for the money - Cadillacs, etc.

     Well, he operated to-day. Took him 50 minutes
to give the woman a spinal (he had previously told
her he would NOT give her a spinal), which should
only take 10 minutes. Then the over-dramatics during the whole remainder of the morning! He was quite
apt at telling me how to handle things up at the
head. But, I fixed him by saying very sweetly, 2 or
3 minutes after, "Were you speaking to me Dr.?" Or
I completely ignored him, entirely. Then he would
ask me how the patient was, and I could honestly
say, "Fine.", and prove it. Perfect ass. I am
thoroughly disgusted that crooked politics can
allow a man like that to operate. He should be in
an institution for addicts, and then should be in
jail for all his criminal abortions!! Honestly, I
cannot understand the public: to be taken in by a
CROOK like him; and a perfect example of degradation
to the Medical Profession. No wonder, some people
don't look too highly upon members of the nursing
and medical prof. with characters in it like this!

     Enough said. Dr. Adams was an angel compared
to this gillygalloot! That's gaelic for son of a B.

     I am going back to my room, now, and take a
bath, and clean up, and will feel more refreshed after,
I know! People like he give me such a bad taste in my
Cerebrum!

     I hate people without principles.

                                        All for now
                                        Earth.

TWO

    After seeing this crack-pot, to-day, I wonder
if I <u>really</u> gave you a true picture of the real Dr.
Adams.

    I don't know where to start.

    But, I will begin: Dr. Adams was a good man.
His kindnesses <u>were</u> genuine; he found out they
could be used, though , to his advantage. He was
sensitive, easily hurt; although he could perhaps hurt people just as badly. (Who can't - with
plenty of experience, - you know, - the good teacher)

    Do you really know the <u>real</u> Sims? He can be
a tremendous agravator; constant, and continual.
Adams had to fight Sims, or Sims would have done *him*
some damage. If Adams hadn't always enjoyed his
medicine, Sims, in his very actions, caused Dr.
Adams to make a better attempt at practicing it.
I am thoroughly convinced that Dr. Adams loved
medicine, although he wasn't astoundingly Grade
A- first class. I'd say, he was Grade A minus-
first class minus - which is pretty damned good,
if you look around the country and see <u>Grade D</u>
doctors practicing red-hot medicine every day!

    He DID have principles!!!!!! I believe
they were born right in him. But, if they were
not, he would just look at his mother, and look
at Sims, and try to be above <u>them.</u> That would
make him better.

    If he realized in the long-run that he
couldn't fool you, and you would say nothing
about it, he respected you for not exposing him,
and worked right along with you, trying his level
best to do his BEST (which was darned good sometimes). He admitted he couldn't give spinals,
and he admitted that he was scared of them.

    When I said in my first letter to you
that he was just a general-run-of-the-mill
genius, I meant it. He caught on to things
when told the first time. He's like me: has
to be shown and guided, rather than get it out
of a book, and attempt it alone, on his own.

    Basically, he was an extremely unhappy
man. Had he had - - well, say an upbringing like
mine: much love, affection and tenderness from two
wonderful, moral, Christian parents; strict training and discipline; being taught the ability to
understand others, and others' misfortunes; to be
happy and content with what you have; to love people
and above all respect and trust them, even tho'
sometimes at your own expense (but, it's a
good teacher), well, had he had that, one might
have found a really, exceptionally fine, fine, person.

--- above reproach, honest, impeccable, etc. etc.
Believe me, I know!! Dr. Adams was a drop in the bucket compared
to this B-S-A-D (can you figure it out?).

If the wife shoots him again, and hits, I'll help you
write this book, too. Brother, it ought to be fun, uncovering all the stuff Brooks has tried to cover up.

He couldn't get a surgeon to help him this A.M.
Finally, a Dr. Ed. Couch (whose wife is a drug addict)
from Winfield, said he would help him., after Dr.
Brooks begged him on the phone. These Drs. just won't
assist him; and I don't blame them!!

Well, I guess I had better run along for now.
I'll be glad when I see you again. I am looking forward
to it, very much.

Will sign off on the other page.

one

He had a sale on his farm, summer of '51, I think it was. He fully expected 500 to show up. I guess maybe 200 came. He had large kettles of chicken and rice mixed together (I forget the southern name for it), and lots of good food. There was much left over. Much waste. The sale did not go off as well as he expected, either. Things were auctioned for terribly small prices, and he laughed it off, as: "Well this spreads good stock amongst the poor farmers, here who ordinarily couldn't possibly buy it." That, was the purpose of the sale, he said. Well, methinks something else. Yes, I think he had a lot of pure-bred stuff; but, I also think he bred anything to anything, and named it "pure-bred". And, it simply wouldn't sell on the really good market. That could possibly be. Sure, he was spreading some better stock around than those farmers were ever used to, but I don't think it was pure-bred. Oh, they had papers, and all their pedigree, but I don't think they were HONEST purely bred stock.

He used to say that when Sonny was at school, somewhere (?) he sent home for some money, and Dr. A. wouldn't send it to him. Like father, like son, - from away back. Anyway this one time he sent him some and when it reached its' destination, Sonny was in California with Johnny Mack Brown's daughter, at their ranch. So, he said, Sonny and Johnny Mack Brown'd daughter were very close. Look into this.

The same man had a pretty good and reliable routine. He generally made rounds at the hospital every morning at 7:45. Hardly ever deviated. Except, of course, on surgical mornings, he started operating at 8:00 (I know). And between operations and after operations, made rounds. He could spot things very quickly. Didn't take him 5 seconds deciding what to do. In other words, he'd look at a case, and say, give so and so, and thus; or, you can go home to-day. "But, Doc, I don't feel well enough to go home. I still feel weak." "Well, you're going home, because you've run the length of your sickness, and you're well enough to go, and no-one but a damn fool like Sims or some other bum would keep you in here any longer. And what's more y' ain't got the money, and I ain't a gonna pay fir your hospital bill. I paid your last one." And he probably had. But, he likely got it back three times over since. Generally the patient would go home, and not reluctantly. With considerable peace of mind. He could talk anybody (nearly) into anything. He had trouble talking other ideas into my head, and he knew it; and by golly, I think he respected me for it. He was always in his office at 10:00 every morning! If it was 5 after 10, we could get alarmed. If he was going to be later, which was seldom, he called the girls to let them know. Between 12:30 and 1:00 the office was deserted and the lights turned off, and all the doors left open for any patient to come in and sit and rest until everybody got back. At two, things started swinging again. Near 4:30 it would ease off to almost nothing, and at 5:00 I came on duty, until 10:00. Here is what I did:
(1) As he would leave the office at 5:00 P.M., he would fastly dictate histories and physicals to me, and letters he expected me to type and have ready for his signature at 10:00. Too fast to write it down. At first it was horrible, and I didn't get all; but he never balled me out. He would give me the data at 10:00 and I'd do it then. But, later on I got so I remembered. I don't know how, but I did. I could have 10 histories and physicals done; three to four letters (business: farm, drugs, political etc.)&(hospital, or hospitalization). I gave shots to the patients who received shots only. This saved him precious time in the day-time, if they could come by at night to get their shots. Like, a minister's widow periodically got asthma shots. Another ministers' wife got liver and B12 shots once a week. Another woman would get estrogen once a week, etc. etc. He never charged ministers, their wives or families. I was often bored because there was so little to do, but, I read a great deal, and knit, and painted.(art). Also painted parts of the office. Also cleaned up a lot. As I have mentioned before. There was plenty of that to do, as they left the place like a madhouse when they left at night. Generally alway he was back once or twice between 5 and 10. To sign letters, or to send out cheques, or to do some business and he said he liked my sharp mind on it. That was another compliment from him.

Also, other than Thelma Curry, I was the smallest one in the office and could
get around quicker. Also, I cleaned things up after I went to work there. There
is a little closet there in the centre of everything, with a hole in the ceiling
for light, that was a fire trap. And dusty!!!!! I never saw such a mess in all my
born days. I cleaned it , lock, stock and barrel. And what he didn't want he sorted
and we threw out. I said to him,"Untidy and messy surroundings means an untidy and
messy mind, and that doesn't seem like you, now does it?" And, he said "No". But
I had angered him a little by saying it, but he was neater afterwards. That closet
was for all the writing paper, envelopes, and forms for sending bills out on, etc.
I put them all in neat rows, and piles, and labelled everything. He appreciated it.
Because he could go in there and never have to ask for anything like he did before.
He could see it and put his hands right on it.

If he didn't make it back during 5 and 10, he usually made it at 10. If
he didn't even make it at 10. he generally called from the hospital, and I gave him
the list of telephone calls that came in, and the outcalls people wanted him
to make, or messages of any and all sorts. Anyway, he was nearly always at the hospital
to make rounds at 10:00 P.M. The nurses hardly complained at his coming in
at that late hour waking the patients. It's a wonder. But, he had many O.B.'s, and
if patients were asleep, he would ask the nurse how they had been, what their
complaints were,etc. And the O.B.'s, if they were in labor, what did it matter. And
if they were asleep, what did it matter, they'd be awakened for feeding their infant so
what difference did it make. And, he had many critical patients that required constant
vigil. His home so near the hospital was the handiest thing. Mrs. Adams said, he
stripped everything off at night, so he could sleep comfortably, and would put on
pyjamas. But you could call him to come to the hospital at 12:30 (that would be
the time you talked with him in bed over the phone) and at 12:35 he would saunter in th
he building looking fresh as a daisy. I believe Mrs. Adams must have laid all his
fresh clothes out for him every night. In a way, he was very fussy about his person.
His office looked like hell I know, but EVERY morning he looked like he stepped
out of a band-box. I don't believe he had a colored shirt to his name; all white.
On surgical mornings he would wear his operative clothes over. He kept them at home,
and paid for the laundering of them because no one wore his big, pot-bellied size
and it was handier to have them right at his finger-tips.

They say he paid to get votes. I'LL BET HE DIDN'T. He never paid to get anythin
I don't know how a man could have so much power, and not pay for it, and he never   (g.
promised anything either!

He used to say, "If I like a person, there isn't enough I can do for them."
And in his own way he meant it. If he liked you he liked you. If he found out he
could fool you, or take advantage of you, or you were a damn fool and got under his
feet, he didn't like you. And to finish, "If I don't like a person there isn't
enough I can do against them, nor the time to do it in." And, brother, he meant
it. He was completely ruthless. Nothing, absolutely nothing got in his way. It
reminded me of the sea that opened, in the bible, and let those tribes cross thru'
(I know my bible like any other heathen) without drowning or getting wet. *Everybody*
just got out of he way & let him go thru' ——— *except Sims &*
He picked things up quickly. In learning, I mean. And, I DID teach *Hastie*
him a lot. I gave him what knowledge I had about anesthesia. Just as the days
passed by. In talking and discussing. And, in certain tecnique over an open
abdomen. I had seen surgery at County during my course, and any time I could
help him improve over anything he was doing, I helped. He had a burn patient in
hosp. for a year. I forget her name at the present. Finally one day, I said
"Let me dress Ethel. Let me do her for you." I took her back to the operating room
every day, and dressed her burns under strict sterile tecnique; and each day, the
purulent material cleared up more, and she healed quicker. Even Sims was frequently
my audience, and he marvelled (which he probably wouldn't admit, now) and complimented
me, and said, "Goddam Adams is lucky" and would walk out.She went home sooner then exp.

Three

Harry T. Ried is the name of the funeral director in Jasper that embalmed Dr. Adams body. I don't know just what Harry T. will tell you. Maybe Dr. Adams was an addict? I don't know. If he was, he wasn't a mainliner, because his viens were not scratched.

I can't think of too much else at this time that is of any importance.

Don't let Sims tell you Adams started all the addiction in Live oak. Many a time, Sims went up to the nurses' residence and shot their arms full of intravenous nembutal to make them sleep, after he took some of their tail; excuse the crude way of putting it. But, one of the nurses' told me that. Then she left Live Oak; she couldn't stand the ethics existing.

Be careful when you enquire about Dr. Adams getting a gun. I imagine I am the only one that knows (maybe Mary does) he ordered one. It was $$$$$$$ discussed with me by Houston Roberts in the strictest of confidences; AFTER his death. And, I imagine the only reason that I was told, was that I was leaving town for good, and it would be safe to tell me.

A guy named Morrison used to be on the Police Force. He was a sad sack, if there ever was one. I think Adams got him fired. Then he'd mope around Adams' office asking theDr. for favors, and Dr. Adams would treat him kindly, but he hated his guts. Morrison never knew how Dr. Adams hated him. In fact, niether did Jean Hart know how she irritated him. But, his objective was to get as many people to like him as was possible. And, so he would not show his likes and dislikes too freely. There was a short, fat orderly, named John. (colored). Lived behind the hospital in an old unpainted house. His wife used to have migrane headaches. She used to get a lot of Demerol. Dr. Adams shipped her off to Jax to a brain specialist, and I believe the story he spread around Live Oak was that she had a brain tumor. Whether it was true or not I don'tknow .

Have you looked up this Mrs. Florence Hagan? I don't know what she may know. She may shoo you off the place with a 45! She's a grass widow; lives with an "adopted" son Troy Skipper. She keeps him ignorant, to keep him on the farm, working for her. He told me once that there were two things he would like to be: either a minister, or a doctor. What a difference! He'll never be anything, but what he is.

Mr. Culpepper, Live Oak druggist (has the Live Oak Drugstore), may talk, but probably very little. He is very quiet and stutters if he doesn't know you. He seems to be shy.

Jake Kennon (Home Pharmacy) got mad at Dr. Adams one day. Because Dr. Adams told Mrs. Kennon that she was neurotic and would feel better if she took a prescription of barbiturates until she got rested up from being so nervous; which was the truth. Kennon's came to Live Oak with nothing.In less than a year they had this beautiful, gorgeous home on Pine St., and a station wagon, and a new Chrysler, etc., etc., etc. But they admit it.

Hunter's Pharmacy. I think old man Hunter is an old reprobate. I never liked him; just from natural instinct. He's not up on his drugs; half the time doesn't know what you're asking for when you go in for it. He practices a lot of Doctoring over the counter himself.

Dr. Adams put Wes. Mizell (feed store), alcoholic, on Antibuse. And, unless Wes. is on it again, he cured him. Hurrah! He drank something awful. And if you know anything about Antibuse, it can scare a patient into not drinking! Wes tried drinking ONCE while he was on Antibuse, and he wound up in the hosp. so sick, and nearly dead; but he had been warned by Dr. A. what would happen.

Four

That happened in the spring, I think of 1952. Wes. wasn't drinking at the time of Dr. Adams death, nor after, when I was down there visiting. It had been about 8 or 9 months since he had had a drink. Three cheers for Wes.; and for Dr. Adams.

Dr. Adams had to give a lecture at the Public Health department one day. He asked me to prepare his speach 30 minutes before he was to speak. I nearly died. "How do you expect to give a speach that isn't even written yet?" He said, "I'll read it. You write it". So, I did, while he was making outcalls at noon, and I was in the car with him. I made him memorize everything I wrote down, in between the latest prices of hogs, and the diagnosis of the last patient we had called on. He was purposely trying to aggravate. As we pulled up to the Health Dept., I said "Do you know what we are going to speak about - I'll have to prompt you ". "The Hell you will. Gimme that paper. It's about Germ Warfare, or something,"and on and on he went, and he was quite right . And it came off without a hitch, and the dumb Health Department enjoyed it!!

He was insecure about something. I think it goes back to his childhood and that false, non-loving mother he had. Actually, I think they were identical. Mary, he didn't like. He loved the sister in Tallahassee. His mother has a cruel mouth and is very deceitful. She had her face lifted in the early part of '52, and one day in the office when we were discussing it, Dr. Adams opened the back door and spit - "Those are my sentiments", he said. Mrs. Wilson said, to me, "He doesn't like his mother It was quite obvious.

(his sister)

I think he did an abortion on a Chitwood girl The Chitwood boy married a Raechel somebody, a nurse that Sims used to run around with. Gladys Chitwood. That is her name. They have cabins and a store out on the east side of Live Oak. Sims used to run around with a Catholic nurse named Kay Trottier, now Mrs. Sonny Hurst, living in the Sherwood Forest part of Live Oak. Near Mrs. Hurst lives another Chitwood girl, named Mrs???? They live next door to the vacant lot next to Dr. Sims. Kay had to get married. Dr. Sims stated that they might have to do a section because if the baby went to full term it would endanger the mother's and the baby's life. That was a blind. The baby weighed about 9 lbs. a day or two after Sims said that, when it was delivered normally, without forceps, even. Kay had been running around with Sims, and he dropped her, and she got caught with Sonny, I guess, because she really is better than he is. He has a farm, and he also bull-dozes. It is not the life that Kay was raised for, and she is very unhappy. She writes to me frequently; I feel sorry for her. She is likeable. She'll eventually find some happiness there, though. He loves her, I think, and will get her anything just about, that she wants.

Dr. Adams felt the depth of Sonny's death. But, he also used it as a way to get people's sympathy to get votes. Don't think he didn't. I could see it! They'd come in and start sympathizing, and he would shed honest tears, then they would say, "Well Doc, it ain't much, but the least I can do, is vote for you." He would thank them, and say, "Well, I was a-countin' on you anyway. You've always been afriend of mine, you know." He used it to get votes; and I'll bet he got a lot more too, as a result of it.

Incidentally, if at any time you wire me anything, naturally you would have to send it in my name. Wire it from Lake City - NOT Live Oak. Or any other large city you may be in at the time would be O.K.(You mentioned wiring me a plane ticket.)

I used to help Mrs. (Dr.) Workman teach at the Air Patrol, or whatever it is called. We taught first aid; home nursing, etc. It was interesting. In rooms up above the Home Pharmacy.

I am at a loss to think of anything else to say. I feel that I have let you down this trip. However may think of something in the future.

HOPE THIS JUNK WILL BE OF SOME HELP, WILL THINK OF SOME MORE.

Page One B ⑪ ①

Six feet, two inches tall. Two-hundred and seventy pounds in weight. Gray hair, (turned grayer after sons' death in February, 1952) parted in the middle. Brown, kind, sensitive eyes. Fat cheeks and jowels. Generally always clean-shaven. No hair about ears, ear-lobes. Eye-brows plucked in centre, over nose. Thick, fat, creased neck. Also, short neck. Much hair around back of neck, shoulders, back, arms, chest (could be noted in hospital scrub suit). Short, fat hand, not too long. Nails generally always clean, and mostly always manicured with colorless nail enamel. Neat and trim, of about 1/16 in. length. "Pot" belly started almost directly out from collar-bone, to the size of a LARGE 10 months pregnancy. Trousers held up by belt; not suspenders. Top of trousers never came up to "natural waist-line" (as called in dress designing) but below curvature of abdomen. All belly and no hips - a direct quote of his son-in-law. Small hips. Long legs. I suppose average size male shoe. Usually slip ons., not tied shoes with laces. WOULD WEAR UNTIL HOLE IN SOLE.

Subject had occasional bouts of asthma, by which, I went to tell when he was extremely upset, or under terrific strain. Bouts were rare. Wheezed occasionally (no relationship to asthma) or rather frequently, which was due to, I believe more than anything else, his extreme obesity, and the speed by which he did everything.

Was sometimes known as the "shot doctor". No patient left his office without a shot. Anyway with most of those natives getting acquainted with medicine and a new hospital, of which most of them were afraid, it was as good a way as any to get them used to the idea that medicine wasn't just herb tea. Most of the shots were inexpensive, injectable vitamin compounds (Miami Pharm.) which wouldn't hurt the best of us, and penicillin. Lots of the pain those natives had was the pain of lost hope and despondency; and believe me, I'd see them later say, "Doc. you don't know how that medicine helped me. I'll drop by for some more sometime". In other words, when he felt down again, he'd drop by and see the "Doc", get a shot (of that there magic stuff) & feel like new again for awhile.

His desk was always in a mess. Papers everywhere; but he knew where to find it all. He could go in, in the dark of night put his hand on the desk and nine times out of ten come out with the right slip. Didn't even look to be sure, get to his destination, and hand over the correct slip to whoever was waiting. Incredible, but true. I've seen it happen. Go with him to turn the light on, and he'd bump slam into me coming BACK WITH the paper in his hand. I tidied his desk up one day, which was the way it stayed from then on, and the wall behind him I attached charts which held his Hampshire Hog papers and records, his hospitalization forms, etc. He could never find anything quick enough from that day on. It seems that his brain memorized where he lay, or placed things. Not where they were supposed to be kept - some place in order.

One day, my sole job was to name (registered names) over two hundred Hampshire hogs; starting to run out of names (on the registery forms,) I finally put the last few down as Madam Edith M. (after me), Miss Tachy Cardia, Miss Cola Sis Titus, & Dr. John M. (latter after Dr. Sims). When he saw the name of the last one,"I'm going to drown that bastard; it's a runt anyway." And grinned all over. We all knew what he meant. And I did it just to get a rise out of him because he hated Sims so.

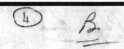
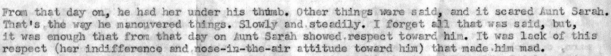

From that day on, he had her under his thumb. Other things were said, and it scared Aunt Sarah. That's the way he manouvered things. Slowly and steadily. I forget all that was said, but, it was enough that from that day on Aunt Sarah showed respect toward him. It was lack of this respect (her indifference and nose-in-the-air attitude toward him) that made him mad.

Look up the colored undertaker. There are two. The short, well built, fairly good-looking one, ~~black~~, not too black, with some freckles, I think. He used to show up at Dr. A's office often during the week, with MUCH money that he handed to Dr. I guessed it was bolita money. Sometimes the wad was 4 inches thick, large denomination bills. I certainly was not to have seen them, and when I showed up at the wrong time, some fast exchanging of hands, and shoving into the pockets was done. I never batted an eyelash, nor enquired later, but just went about my business, as if I were a "wee bit simple." After all I guessed immediately what was going on, and I knew better than ever ask.

The Klu Klux Klan meets in an unused (I believe unused) white frame clap-board church, down near Branford, every Monday night without fail. That was an excellent source of information for Dr. Adams. Not only that, many things were planned there. That was the information part of it. Sims and Haskell want to join; will not be accepted. They'll never let them in. What Sam Gibbs and Seward Fleet wouldn't give to know where they meet and when. They'd TRY,.... to do something about it.

~~Sims~~ During my stay in Live Oak, there was one great, grand, and glorious parade with the Grand Dragon, etc. etc. etc, many were from N. and S. Carolina, Georgia, and little old Live Oak was well shown! About a year later there was a burning of a cross out across from old man Blue's place. It was a hideous looking sight. I asked Dr. Adams if he went,.. (innocently, not knowing, then, that he was a member)..."What were they burning? Who was burning it? A cross, you say? The Klu Klux Klan? Didn't know there was any". Then, he immediately changed the subject.

One night Mary, and I, and he were coming home from Mayo, having made an outcall. He deliberately hit a hound dog with his car (Red Olds.) on the road. It frightened me for a minute, and the cruelty didn't leave me for a long time. Because, he deliberately swerved over to hit it on purpose. Laughed, and said, "The Goddamned thing was in the way on the road". I'll bet you a dollar he knew who owned it, and had a grudge against them. Of course we would never know. Mary Bawled him out. Or then it may have been some immature, childish act.

He frequently went out to eat with old man Blue . Free, of course.

One day Mrs. Sheffield called from the hospital & asked for Dr. Adams. I said, "Just a minute". Went out to the curbing where he was in a car talking with some man. "Mrs. Sheffield wants to talk with you". "Ask her what she wants". Back to the phone, and she said, "I just want to talk to Dr. Adams. Will you please get him for me?". I had lots of time, and I had a fair idea of what was going to eventually happen, so I figured I could have some fun. Out to the car again. "She's still on the wire. Wants to talk to you. I won't do". "Ask her what she wants". He was a little annoyed, but not much. Back to the phone, "He's out in a car at the curbing, & won't come in. He wants to know what you want". "I, WANT, TO, TALK, TO, DR, ADAMS!!! That's what I want". So, I slammed the receiver up on her, went out and told Dr. Adams what she had said, and what I HAD done. He shook his head, and said, "O.K. Fine." The phone rang again. Mrs. Sheffield. Most of the time she talked in a low, masculine, monotone - very lifeless like. This is what she was using, to-day. "Miss Park. I want to talk to Dr. Adams, not you. I have a fractured wrist

① ② ℬ ③

I don't think Sims was in town 5 minutes when Sims said, "I'll have this town in less than 6 months, because Adams isn't qualified to do what he is doing; and I am. And I will run him out of town". After I started working for Sims I heard that often.

What he didn't know was that Adams had been working breathlessly for ages to get the people to like him for political reasons as much as any, and he wasn't going to have some young blade come in and toss him around. Apparently someone ran and told Adams what Sims had said, and from that day on the fued began. Although at first they did some surgery together; but not when I knew them. Either of them, with the proper training would have been hard to beat.(Sims can lie, too. Many a time Dr. Russell Counts had done a Gastric Resection, and Sims took all the credit in front of the patient, and told the patient he had done it and never mentioned Dr. Counts' name.) Sims has more training than Adams, but not a hell of a lot more. Somehow on other he tries to do better medicine than Adams. Better tecnique, better office and equipment. He's making his money out of medicine; Adams made it other ways. But, they are both after money. Sims favorite quote," I believe in every luxury available to mankind, and I intend to have them. I do NOT believe in any form of self-deprivation!" And he looked like a millionare, while his wife looked like a ninth-rate whore, and the four kids were all the time sniffling around her heels like flies on a sticky summers' day, snot running out of their noses a mile a minute, coughing and wheezing with asthma, and the baby, ~~bar~~ Larry already addicted to barbiturates because of infant exzema. He was just covered with open scabs and scars of exzema and they kept him completely doped on ~~probably~~ probably (eventually) 20 grains of barbiturate daily.

I've told you this last for comparison. Don't let Sims fool you; he'll try.

For a tall, big man, Dr. Adams voice was high, not low and booming like one might imagine. Sometimes, for fun, he'd answer the p one (never know who it would be)) and in a very high voice pretend he was one of the girls at the office. And if it was someone he didn't want to talk to, or see, he'd just say, "I'll tell the doctor to come down right away. Good-bye". He'd not go near them, and the next day, he'd say, "I didn't get a message at all. I'm sorry." He knew they didn't need to see him; and what's more he didn't want to be bothered with them. Sometimes I'd call the office from the apartment, and Mrs. Wilson would answer. I'd want to talk with him.~~&Mrs&~~ I'd hear Mrs. Wilson say it's Miss Park. He'd say, "Watch this". " Hello". "Hello Dr. Adams,..... ". He would interupt, "I'm sorry but this is the funeral home", and hang right up on me. I'd call right back, and the first thing I'd hear after the phone went off the hook, "Suwannee Funeral Home". Click. After the third attempt I'd nearly always get results. You never knew when he was going to pull stunts like that. But, one thing you never had to worry about when he was going to lose his temper, because he lost it so very rarely. (Once, with me, in my two years of working there.) (About the income tax form I told you about.)

He was a fast worker, and a hard worker. No grass grew under his feet. Speed counted in that office, & ALL OVER., INCLUDING THE FARM.

Thelma was terribly untidy in her work (colored Thelma). Mrs. Wilson's name is Thelma, too. Thelma talked about sex a lot. Too much to suit me.

Mrs. Wilson was untidy about her person; her work was a little untidy too; but after I went there to work, she made honest efforts to improve. I don't think she had had the basic training. Nearly every night after I left the office, I had thoroughly tidied the whole joint. During my stay there, I painted the lavatory (white) ← THE WHITE LAVATORY laboratory, put white curtains on the lab shelves, at my own expense.

Sometimes he and Mary and I would make some outcalls with him, if it was after work (after 10:00P.M.) for me. He'd go miles out in the woods, take out his bag, go into the house, or shack, sit down, visit, eat, -then diagnose and treat!

16   ③   ⒷＢ   4

Not hardly the routine a real doctor takes; but to those people, probably the best
tecnique to use. They have no tolerance with the real professional-acting man. They think
he is a snob. The people of Suwannee County complain of Dr. Workman, Sims and Black of
being snobs. TOO PROFESSIONAL.

Watch what you say TO Haskell; he's dirtier than Adams ever thought of being;
although isn't as crooked, tho' would like to be, but lacks the guts. Looking at people
like him, makes me think that when he was born, they threw away the baby, and kept the
placenta. Or, had they done that, they might have had a better specimen.

If you're smart, you'll make him look dirty in this book; because any other way
would be false. Even Sims will tell you that; but Sims cannot say much, because he
has to work with him. But, he told me that, the time he apologized to me. Sims hates
Haskell like Adams hated Workman. He used him. Look up Workman (West Palm, or Palm
Beach). He left there in a great big hurry. Some unethics, somewhere (Excuse my spelling of
descriptive words). In Live Oak, he killed a boy named Griffin, during anesthesia
induction. Absolute carelessness, and arogance. Look for those legal records if you can. That
would be a hospital chart; maybe you can't get it. I forget the boys' full name. The boys'
grandmother lives north and west (a very little) of a Mr. and Mrs. H.S. Wright. Enquire
of this old grandmother. A MR. Griffin, post-office worker, and pretends to be a n
Advent church minister (part-time), is an uncle to the boy. A Mrs. W.E. Ambrose, my former
land-lady, 406 East Duval St., is a mother-in-law to a cousin of the the Griffin boy. I
think it's cousin, maybe it's brother. This daughter-in-law of Mrs. Ambrose lives in
Jacksonville; but, the name is not Ambrose; Mrs. Ambrose was married several times.
This particular son, I believe owns a junk yard on the edge of Jacksonville city limits:
Butler, it just came to me; on Hwy.# 90 as you go in from the west to Jax. Ravis
Butler, I think it is. Well, you may get something rich there; or maybe mostly malice,
but this daughter-in-law was going to sue Dr. Adams for manslaughter. And Dr. Workman
too, I believe.

Once Sims had a ruptured ectopic case, and while in the belly did a
thorough exploratory, appendectomy, took a slice out of the uterus to send away to see if it
was fibromatous, sewed her up, and she died of internal hemorrhage, after 19 pints of
blood. I was working for Adams at the time. The operation was in the A.M.; she died in the
P.M. The family went to Keith Black , to sue Sims for Manslaughter. As far as I know, Dr.
Adams said," refuse," and tell the people they can't gain anything by it." He said to me, if
news like that ever hit the Associated Press, where in the hell would Suwannee County be,
Medically? We have got the American Medical Association to think of too. Now I can see, he did
really mean that. Only, he did not want people in there inspecting, and finding things out about
HIM! You know, had things been reversed, Sims would have had someone in; he wouldn't
have been smart enough to realize they wouldn't just look into Adams, but every Dr. Black did
a crim. abor. on the daughter of Mrs. Whitfield, who works for Sims. The daughter died of
hemorrhage, only seconds after her admittance to Suw. Co. Hosp. Dr. Adams stood behind
Black, then. This was before my time in Live Oak. Of course, he then had his thumb right on
Dr. Black.

IDE AT HOSP→Mrs. Ruby Bullard, lives north of Live Oak, on Hwy. to Jasper and off to right,
is a Demeral addict. Gets the stuff from the hospital?? I've wondered about Helen Dunkel???

Look up J.C. Fletcher, JR., or his divorced wife who I think lives in Live Oak.
Miss Sarah Stalnacher, "dietician", is a hamburger-joint-whore. Goes with the guy that runs the
John-Dere section of the Farmer's Hardware. He's married. She's gone with Fletcher, Jr., Sims,
Haskell, Counts, Reece Brown, and others too numerable too mention. She'll stab you in the back,
with a sweet, motherly smile on her face. She had it in for Dr. Adams, until one day Dr. A.
pulled one on her. Jacque Collins was a friend of Sims, and "Aunt" Sarah's (as they call her)
Dr. A. finally got Milliken to go out with Jacque, steadily. Then one day at the table, in the
hosp. dining-room, Dr. A. asked Jacque who the party was at the hospital that was going with this
John-Dere man (I forget his name... Elmer something). Of course he knew. Aunt Sarah alerted.

(circled numbers at top: ⑦ ⑤ B 5)

patient out here, I want him to see. Will you tell him please". I said, "Yes, I will".
Didn't hang up, went out & told him, he said, "Tell her to send it down here to the office".
I delivered his message. Mrs. Sheffield said, "Miss Park, is Dr. Adams there? I want to send
this patient down to him to take care of, not to you!" I said, "Yes, he is. I can't get
him to come in". She said, "I want to speak to Dr. Adams." I went out again, and told him all.
He got out of the car, his face was purple-red with rage; he said quietly to the man, "I'll be
right back, don't go away". He said to me, "Go in and hang up on that goddamned bitch". He
went over to the service-station, and called the hospital, just frothing at the mouth. The
service station attendent told me the next day, "Boy, that's the first time I've ever seen
Doc.mad. And I hope it's the last. When he finally got who he was calling, he said,'Goddammit,
you stupid whore, you want to talk to me, now, Goddammit talk. When I git through. When I tell
my office nurse to tell you to have any patient sent down to my office, I don't want any sass
or back-talk from you or anyone else. Now, Goddammit, you send that patient down here to my
office right now, and not another word out of you. And, don't you ever keep on bothering me,
when someone tells you I am talking to someone". And he hung up. The nurses at the hospital
wanted to know what happened because, they said Mrs. Sheffield sobbed for what seemdd like hours
in her office, and when she came out her eyes were red, and she was as white as a ghost, and
unnaturally quiet. It was a horrible way to speak to any woman; but she acted like that all the
time. Sometimes she nearly drove us crazy in the office. I felt so sorry for her.

I don't know all the details of her being put in jail for drug addiction. I was
never aware she was a drug addict. But, I think maybe, she, or between she, and Dr. A., that was
how Ruby Bullard got her Demerol . Far too many times, Mrs. Sheffield & Ruby Bullard came out
of the windowless, one-doored drug-room of the hospital, chit-chatting. Ruby was always gay after
that. Possibly Mrs. Sheffield gave Ruby an ampoule or two, at Dr. Adams order or request, each
day??? Then Ruby stole the rest. If a patient got 50 mgms. there would be 50 mgms. left in the
ampoule. It would disappear. Always after Ruby had been seen in that vicinity. I don't know
what Mrs. Martha (Lamar) Simms could tell you. I don't think Mrs. Margaret Sapp of Jasper
will talk much. Dr. Adams claimed he put Dr. Hiram Curry through school (Jasper). You might look
into that. You say you haven't seen or found J.J. Elliott at all? Watch him. He'll pretend to
be Jesus Christ himself. He's got an aortic aneurysm, which 90% of the time means incurable
syphilis. In fact we just consider they have it, when that is present.(He doesn't know.) He's
beginning to show very minute signs of 4th stage syphilis, already. They are not noticeable to
to lay-eye; hardly to the professional eye.

A nurse by the name of Bennye Isam ......, I forget her married name. If she
is still in Live Oak, may give you some malicious stuff. Maybe something helpful, I don't
know.

Miss Laveta Trim (the girl whose apartment I called for ages that one night)
is now married, and living in Lake City, I think. Possibly to a Hwy. Patrolman. Her sister,
married, too, Lavonne, works for Dr. Sims. They are nieces of this Mrs. Whitfield.
The Ed. Kent family, and the Forrest Bradbury family are very close to the Dr. Sims. Theyare
100% enemies of mine; their choice. Mrs. Loy Perry (a second wife) was disappointed in her
first marriage because, as good as her husband was in bed, and Social Prestige - so she has said
he went out on her too much, and she couldn't stand it, so divorced him. Came to Suwannee
County as Home Economics Demonstrator. Loy was just a new widower. She got him to build a beautiful home on Pine St., and married him, she told me, because, he was quiet, and she felt he
would never go out on her. But, Doris played around muchly, with Dr. Sims; then Loy got her
pregnant. She wanted a baby. Not many knew, if any, that she went with Sims. Mrs. Bradbury, a sister of Loy Perry lives across the street. The Bradbury's were having a big party, one night to which Loy's
had not been asked. Apparently Sims made an outcall, sneaked back quietly, parked his car at
Bradbury's, went in to Doris' and had some, but not before I saw them at it! Everyone knows that
Doris stays up late reading because she doesn't like sleeping with Loy. I left Dr. Adams office a
at 10:00 P.M., and wandered over to Doris Perry's. It was a good thing I went to the usual door,
and not to the front to ring the door-bell. It would have awakened Loy. I waited about 10 damn
long minutes before I knocked, after Sims had gone. Doris was quite happy but, I think she
wondered how close I was, although I told her I had walked over slowly. No one knows about this,
but, once Dr. Adams said, "If Doris Perry had 'em sticking out of her, like she's had 'em
sticking in her, she'd look like a porcupine." Doris Perry had the misfortune to have
a baby that borders on the idiot side. The baby must be two years old, nearly, but I don't
think it even sits up, yet. Her whole reproductive system has undergone a lot of G.C. infections.
Her history proves that. Also reading a chart that I wasn't supposed to, helped.

INCIDENTALLY, LOY HAS GONE OUT ON HER INEVER FELT SO SORRY
FOR ANYONE, AS THE DAY SHE TOLD DOROTHY HARRIS & I THAT.

A// (13)   Page ①   ①

"Gawd Almighty Damn," he bawled.   "Oh-h, I ain't so much," he'd drag out, upon
being asked, "How are you to-day, Doc?". Everyone, nearly called him Doc. He
just loved it. Nothing fancy, For Him. He respected my professional attitude
and I was flattered, because I thought he would scoff at it, perhaps. He knew
his medicine, as if by magic, and, believe me he knew his Medical ethics, or
Professional ethics, better than a lot of these thin- assed bastards around here;
even tho' they'd been asked hundreds of times by the D.A. to stick it. ←   *I often referred to him as the D A (initials)*

      He loathed stupid women! And, what's more, so did I. And, do.
He became red-mad if his word was doubted, or if the word of any of his employees
was doubted, especially Mrs. Wilson, and I. (Fracture: Mrs. Sheffield, office,
service station)."Any employee of mine is PROTECTED. I'm a big enough man to do
so, too".

Page 4 & 5-B.   "Niggers, and Yankees and dogs are all in the same class". "What does
that make me, then?", I asked him. "You're a Canadian, aren't you? Well what're
you asking for?You ain't a damn Yankee, your skin's white and you only walk on 2
legs!"

      Stomping in in the morning to work,brisk, fast, on the ball. I didn't
know how 270 lbs. could travel so fast. We moved in the A.M. We moved all day!
He didn't try to be the fastest, but he was one of the fastest operators I have
ever seen. His brain never rested.   ←   *also in surgery.*

      The night his dau. was in labor, he lay down on a bed at the end of the
corridor, and in less than 100 seconds he was snoring so loud we had to waken
him, so he would not disturb the other patients. He got up mumbling, went back
to an O.R. stretcher in the O.R. forer and snored to his hearts' content.
      He was mussy, and untidy, but clean and neat. Can you figure that
one out? Always had a hole in his right sock, right where his big toe would come
out. Politics. He probably had 5 doz. NEW pairs at the house!
      He despised weak-livered men. And he used them, and they didn't
even know it. He'd put his arm around some yellow-livered SOB and call him Pal,
, and as soon as his back was turned would spit on the ground."Help that sunnofa-
bitch? Iwouldn't help him dig his own grave, even if I thought it would help him
get in it sooner!" They never knew. That is kindness, They never guessed.
                    I GUESS.

A// (1) (2) (2)

I'VE SEEN MILLIKEN SHAKING IN HIS BOOTS, HE'S BEEN SO SCARED — OF WHAT, I DON'T KNOW

The Hiway Pat. was used, too. He was a yellow-livered son of a gun, but he was of use. I knew. He used to go out with Jaque Collins, R.N. Dr. Adams knew and approved. That's how he got his hold on Milliken. Blackmail? You see the hiway patrolman was married.

$50,000 INS

Mary. Blonde, blue-eyed, well filled in, Mary. Left with nothing. He knew. He told her what she was to get if anything ever happened to him. He told me he'd never marry again, if he were ever free again. I never repeated that. I knew Mary would get nothing. I wasn't surprised. I wasn't surprised at anything that ever happened. Because I knew the unusual and rare was always happening. It was wonderful. I had never been so happy in this new world of good, and BAD; so much bad, so often that it almost seemed right. Where did one draw the line anyway between right and wrong? When there was so much wrong, and it seemed right. At least everything always worked out. Except Sonny's death. I told him that was God trying to reach him. He scoffed at me. But, he told Mrs. Wilson I was right, after my back was turned. Then his own death. God couldn't take any more. No one could go on fooling the people and himself so much, anylonger. I never knew an unhappier man. Really unhappy. Down underneath;... no, he didn't care, he laughed, he hurt people, he'd kill an animal on purpose, hitting it with his car, he'd curse a person out, laying them so low- never apologise, hit-and-miss, seemingly carefree, and not caring a hoot; hurting Florrie Lee, really not caring about a solitary thing;—because, he was a pathological liar, and he knew he could lie his way out of it. God caught up with him. I knew him. He never knew I knew him. That was ONE thing he did not know. *I BELIEVE, HE THOUGHT HE FOOLED ME A LOT, IF NOT ALL, OF THE TIME!*

Anti-social ... he was anti-social & he claimed to be, but when he was thrust into the middle of a party that he couldn't get out of, no one was more humble, gracious, or polite, or seemed more relaxed or had a better time

SIMS SAYS, "HE IS A COMMUNIST."

③

Dr. Adams used to say, "For every 10 cents I make in the office, I
make $10.00 on the farm." And I think he was right. Except, I think he
made a terrific amount in Bolita money. Too often I saw Charles Hall in
there paying him off, for him to have made only a little bit! One night,
I am sure it was by accident, although he knew I would walk in surely,
he was counting money in a little green box, about 10 X 6 X 4, with a
chrome or aluminum handle on top. Inexpensive looking. It locked with a
key. I didn't say "Boo", or question him in any way. But it was full. I
didn't look too hard either, because I wanted him to trust me, and when I
felt something was not my business, I never pried. But, I know some in
his hand were large denominations. I never saw it again, and I don't know
what he did with it.

After he died, before I went back to Canada, and when I had finished
doing the charts, J.J. Elliott and Mrs. Adams and I went down to the office.
I had to pick up some things of mine. Mrs. Adams stayed in the car. It was
raining. We parked out in front, so I wouldn't get wet. I could slip up on
the sidewalk under that canopy that runs along in front. When Mr. Elliott
got out of his side of the car, and came around to my side to let me out,
Mrs. Adams had time to say, "Leroy kept a very LARGE sum of cash in a box
somewhere;"she continued on fast, for Mr. Elliott was nearly at the door,
"I think it is in between the partitions of the office somewhere, but I
can't get in (without some damn fool) to look for it. I don't know what to
do." I said,"Here's Jeff, we'll talk about it later. The fewer you tell,
the better. DON'T tell anybody!!". We discussed it very lightly again,
before I left, but not much was said, because there was so little to say.
I told her I might be wrong, but I didn't trust J.J. Elliott or Mr. Black
as far as I could throw them. And for her to watch them. I was wondering
if the money was left at the cottage with Mary. He didn't know he was going
to be shot in the back, and maybe kept it out there for safety from the
Internal Revenue. The latter visited him frequently. His bank accounts were
always overdrawn, purposely. Many a time I waited for my pay-check, only a
day or two, until he would deposit some money. I am SURE money was left.
If it was at the cottage then only Mary alone knows it. And is saying nothing.
Mrs. Adams didn't know how much I knew about Mary. She had no idea Dr. A.
had ever discussed it with me. But, the A.M. I left for Canada, after the
funeral, Mrs. A. said, "They got the Ford from that girl; and apparently she
said,'Well, I was surely left without anything. This is not what I expected!!'
To soothe Mrs. Adams I said, "What did she expect when she tried to break
up a marriage, and a home. She's lucky she's got her skin!!". I couldn't say
that her husband was just as much for it as Mary was. Which was the truth,
but why hurt people. Mrs Adams has gone through enough. If Mary had it,
what if, in her haste of losing the car, etc, she blurted out to Jeff, "Well,
I've got his money box, and it's FULL; and I'll not tell anybody." What if
she paid him off to keep quiet? She could do almost anything with it and no
one would know. She could deny anything, and keep on denying. My guess is
that IF she had it, she said nothing. I know I wouldn't say a word! Some of
his shrewdness may have rubbed off on her. It couldn't help. Of course if it
happened to be at the cottage, Black would almost really know about it. Or
would he? This shooting happened in a hurry. Ruby beat him to the draw, only
by days; maybe hours! He didn't calculate on his being killed. If J.J. knew
so fast where Ruby's money was; maybe that was the Dr's., and he had been keeping it there for a day or two to console Ruby; then when he would shoot her, he
could take off with the loot , and who would be the wiser. No one would
DREAM that a white man would have shot Ruby. And certainly not a doctor of medicine, AND NOT DR. ADAMS!!! I feel very sure that there was money left (cash) &
SOMEONE has it; and you nor I nor the Internal Revenue will never know WHO!

④

The night after we had buried Sonny that P.M., some young kid
about 21, and a young girl came to their front door, and wanted a Dr.
to take a wasserman so,they could go,up to Folkston(?) Georgia & get
married. Dr. Adams said to the fellow, "I just buried my only son this
afternoon, and I don't feel like going down to any office to-night. I
want to spend to-night with my family. You'll have to go to someone else."
The guy said, "You're kidding!! You're having a party aren't you? We want to
get married". Well, I was nearly to the door, (the guy was inside, in the
living-room), but I made fast tracks when he said that! I thought Dr. Adams
was going to kill him, with the look he gave him. Then he just looked away,
and said,"Miss Park take care of them." I took them outside the door, and scolded
him for making a remark like that. I said, "People don't joke about burying
only sons. You had no business being so stupid as to say anything like that to
Dr. Adams." I got my purse and went to the office with the boy. We never charged
much for pre-marital wasserman's, but that arrogant S.O.B. never let up about what
a joke it was, his saying that. I knew they wanted to get married. That smart-
alek said, "Doc should have come down; it would take his mind off his misery."
Before I handed him his O.K.'d sheets, (that he had to have, or he couldn't get
married), I said, quietly, "That will be $30.00; $15.00 each." I didn't bat an
eyelash; I looked him straight in the face and eyes, ---. He paid it!! Dr. Adams
grinned when I handed him the thirty dollars. I said,"I saw what they had left
in his wallet. I guess they can buy enough gas to get to Folkston. Then they
can work a day to get the money to pay the judge. Smart Aleck." Dr. Adams just
looked up with tears in his eyes and said, to everybody, "That's my best assistant."
All the other office crew had gone home; so he didn't hurt anyone's feelings by
saying that. He was awfully sick about Sonny's death. Sonny LOVED the farm, and Dr.
Adams was fixing th farm up for Sonny. Not long before his death, and when he was
being better to Mrs. Adams, he spoke often, "Were going to retire, SOON, on that farm.
I'm going to quit medicine, and LIVe for a change. We'll build a little house,
something like we're in now, Florrie and I, and we'll live it up, out there. That
is where I wanted Sonny to be."

He was sitting in a chair saying this

One

(5)

(step-mother & real father)

(1)

I think he — "finer" Jo up once — worked for him — as never had it

stuck in permanent him!

Alpha Jo McMahon, (Mrs.), whose family live near Jasper, in a recently new home. Was an R.N., who used to be on the staff of S. C. Hosp. If Thelma couldn't work for me, when I would want some time off, Jo would. (Like vacations). Jo used to go with a fellow who used to work for Wiley Grantham. I believe he bought her a new Buick (wine, hard-top convertable). Jo's husband was in Korea. Jo had a Cesarean Section for her last baby. It was not necessary; but Jo was married to a Yankee Catholic, whose family was strict; and while in the abdomen, Dr. Adams cut out (not just ligated) Jo's Fallopian tubes, unbeknownst (spelling?) to her husband. No one was to know about it. I guessed about it, and asked Jo about it so matter of factly, that Jo said, "Oh, Park, don't tell a living soul; my hus- band would kill me if he knew. No one is supposed to know!" Any way the husband came home, in the spring of 1952, I think. And the guy from Grantham's got the ditch, and Jo got the car!!! Also, this guy was in debt, due to Jo, pretty far, and, in the fall of 1952, I read in The Democrat where someone on a lonely side- road had tried to kill this fellow (wish I could think of his name). But, the real story is, that he tried to take his own life, and couldn't go through with it. Jo's husband was from New Hampshire, or Boston, or somewhere up there where I believe Catholicism is pretty strong. At any rate her mother- in- law hardly ever gave her any peace. Well, Jo was, and is pretty attractive (enough for Sims), and has a nice warmth to her personality. She's got what it takes. She used to go with Mr. Fletcher the one-time Superintendent at S.C. Hosp. They were in the Navy together, or some- thing. One night, after I was working for Dr. Adams, J.C. Fletcher got pretty high, and was at the hospital, and Mrs. Sheffield & I were in his office with him, and he showed us all these pictures of Jo and he in several warm clinches. He GAVE me some. I must have thrown them out. Any way, I can't find them.

2 children - boy & girl — *wipe out to paper* — *Have parents!*

Jo told me her husband might have suspected that something was done while in the abdomen, because ~~she~~ HE DETECTED- wasn't as scared of getting pregnant as before he went to Korea; but that she never would tell him. I always liked Jo; but one had to be careful what was said around her, because she was awfully smart. One night at Dr. Adams office when we were painting the lab (she and I), she said, out of the blue- trying to catch me unawares, " Sims must have loved you an awfull lot, and fairly worshipped the ground you walked on to fight you like he did; and the feeling must have been mutual because I've never seen any two fight the way you two do, unless something's there." She wasn't any wiser when I got through talking (I don't think). Many people tried to catch me like that. That's why I adopted the attitude of denying it to everybody. Mostly for my own sake, and for his and his wife's.

Dr. Adams asked me once if I thought J.J. Elliott would make a good Superintendent (to take J.C. Fletcher's place). I said, that probably the only person that could stand J.J. would be he himself (Dr. Adams)..I said emphatically, "No!" In the first place he had no administrative ability, also that he would probably steal the hospital blind (all kinds of supplies could be taken to his home in Clearwater - and who would be any the wiser?). I don't know if Dr. Adams continued to have any plans like this after he got elected, or if he began to use J.J. more and more, then, only. Different things Dr. Adams would ask me, and they were many) I would naturally always show the good side, or moral value (or whatever one calls it), and of course a crook can't act well with those things, and maybe he was going ahead thinking of working HIS ORIGINAL IDEAS ~~these things~~ out anyway. He must have planned for a long time, the kicking out of Mrs. Sheffield, and how to accomplish it. I remember when her parents called at his office after the whole thing was over. They were heart-broken. Simple folk, plainly dressed; it was obvious that they had worked hard all their lives, and were proud that they had a daughter that was a director , or superintendent of nurses. Mrs. Sheffield had really tried hard to be a good citizen. But, the longer she stayed in Live Oak the worse things got for her, and the more and more she got herself behind an eight-ball. I guess she depended on Dr. Adams for guidance, and he misguided her all the way, slowly and in a scheming manner. He put on this big bluff for the parents which sickened me, then and there. I knew that he was one guy that could have prevented this had he a mind to do so; and the very fact that it had happened made it look like he had planned it. He was even out

How sorry he was! & What a wonderful girl Mrs. Sheffield was — & that if he hadn't have messed out of town it wouldn't—

6   TWO   ②

of town, conveniently when it happened (Chicago, I think??). I don't know how
much dope she was on or taking, or anything about it. ~~~~, Dr. Counts said
that Sims called him when it happened and wanted to know what to do; that Mrs.
Sheffield was in a frame-up, and I believe Counts said that Sims wanted Counts to
come to Live Oak, and they would get together against Adams: Haskell, Counts,
Sims, Mrs. Sheffield. Mrs. Sheffield was not lazy; she could get on your nerves
because in her real efforts to help you she got right under your feet. In the
emergency room she was absolutely NO GOOD. She got hysterical. I LOVE EMERGENCY ROOM
work. It calls for your best co-ordination, and gray-matter ability. .

*from
Jack
Pierce*

Mrs. Sheffield went with Fred Green, so Dr. Adams said. Everyone knew about it,
I think. Of course Dr. Adams slowly was running her down. He got so he uttered little
remarks against her; a little at a time. Enough to buzz around and start doing her
damage. She tried to be fair with all the doctors, and Dr. Adams wanted everything
to come his way; and nothing to Sims way. Now, I was fighting Sims; but, he could ↗*But, it*
do what he wanted to professionally as far as I cared. I had another way of getting *was a*
at his core. Anyway, I had nursed for 8 years, counting my training, and HAD a *personal*
CANADIAN training of three years, and I figured I was almost smarter than he, in many *fight.*
practical ways. I don't pretend to know more than a doctor, don't misunderstand me.
I had done supervisory work, had worked for a Specialist in Internal Medicine, had
worked in at least half a dozen hospitals, and until I came to U.S., had most of the
time had my nose in a professional book, as Canadian nurses are prone to do. Amer.
nurses rarely refer to their text-books after they get their R.N.(s. And just about
everything Sims would attempt, I could do better and faster (I made it a point to),
and that griped his very soul. And made him admire me more, too. But, Adams wanted
him squelshed (sp.?) entirely!! I wouldn't do that to anybody. When Mrs. Sheffield
was put in J.C. Fletcher's place - holding down the two jobs: Supt. of nurses, AND
Supt. of Hosp. Adams expected all the gravy. But, she was fair, and ended up in jail
with a drug addiction rap. *FOR WHICH I HELD DR. ADAMS DIRECTLY RESPONSIBLE*

Workman said he had treated her in West Palm Beach. Something glandular???
Anyway, she started to get hairy, and her voice changed (huskier). Whiskers all over
her face. Hair on her chest and abdomen. Dr. Adams said she was just covered. He said
that he had on occasion examined her, and saw all the hair. Examined?????? She had to
shave every day. She wore too much rouge. Which made people look at her face all the
more. I believe she was attempting to cover up the shaving, etc., but only drew
attention to the make-up. She always looked like she could stand a scrub brush
and soap wash! Greasy. She bit her nails. She acted too naive. Pretended not to catch
on to jokes, and would say, "Now-w, Dr. Sims." or "Now-w, Dr. Adams."

One night we had a Cesarean Section. We didn't think we would save the baby.
But it was delivered abdominally, and Mrs. Sheffield took it, and started to work on
it. Rescusitating (sp.?) doubling it's legs up, (art. resp'n.), blowing in it's mouth
(CO2 - to make it breath. Dr. Adams asked her in about 4 mins., "Is the baby alive?"
"It's trying to breath", she said. "It hasn't gasped yet,"I said softly to Dr. Adams.
I continued, "It has made no efforet yet ". This, I practically whispered, so as to
not hurt her feelings. When a doctor wants to know a thing he wants to know what is
going on. Not an excuse. "Is that baby breathing, yet?", he asked. "Well, it is
making a feeble attempt,"She said. Dr. Workman mumbled so she could not hear, "That's
like backing up to the next whistle-stop!" Just then the baby let forth a lusty cry.
Dr. Adams said, as he looked up grinning, "I think I just heard a train blow it's
whistle". Well, poor Mrs. Sheffield was out in the cold as to what was going on when
we all started howling at the way things were said. It was very funny at the time.
No one ever did tell her what the joke was, and it bothered her for several days. Beca.
use, I think she thought we were laughing at her in some manner.

I don't know what influence Dr. Adams had on who, regarding Mrs. Sh.
going with Fred Green. Maybe it was something she and FRed hatched up between the two
of them. But, the Klu Klux Klan meetings, every Monday night were where Dr. Adams
no doubt benefitted much. Houston Roberts got so he told me bits of what was going on.
Minor things.

Mrs. Sh. got her divorce, so Dr. A. said, in the early summer of '52.
I guess Kieth Black got it for her.

③

Dr. A. mentioned it to me one day. I didn't even know she was getting one. It was kept quite quiet, which was a good thing. I don't know who got what against who, but, Dr. Workman said that since this change had come over Mrs. Sheffield her sexual capabilities were nil. ?????

When I got the telephone call from my mother in June '52 that my father was dying of leukemia (which later turned out to be false... a general practitioner trying to think he knew it all), I told Dr. Adams all about it. Then showed him the letter from mother. I think he thought it was a plot on my part. Because I told him it looked like I would have to leave. That if Daddy had only a few months to live, that I being the only child should be at home, not 1500 miles away from home. That was WHY I planned my July vacation to go home and see what the situation was. I DID NOT BELIEVE what my mother had told me. If Daddy was dying of Leukemia, then that disease should have shown up in January of 1950, when he had had his surgery for Lymphosarcoma of the rectum!! When they were testing him for everything under the sun. Blood dyscrasias show up under micro's, when making a simple cell count! This news did not hold water, but, anyway I was going home to see. When I got home, things were as I suspected. O.K. I wrote back to Dr. Adams saying I would be back for the winter, anyway. He had plenty of time to get my letter before his death.

But, I was getting restless and wanted to leave him. I was sick and tired of fighting Sims, and a lot of that had died, anyway. I figured I had hurt him enough, and anyway, had I not hurt him by then, I never would, and why waste my time? I was sick of the whole mess.

Dr. Adams had a habit of always saying, "Hey-y-y ---, kid!", with a lilt to his voice, in a very pleasant manner, to everyone. Some of the kids were 2 or 3 years old; but more likely the "kids" were 65 or 70! They just loved it. He had one nice thought: He used to say, "You can speak to EVERYBODY! Just 'cause you speak to them, doesn't mean you associate with them, or have to associate with them!" And, I've seen him be kind, and speak to people, practically go out of his way to do so, that you or I wouldn't bother with, and it would tickle them to pieces!! Then he would go about his business, and I'll bet you if someone asked him the next day if he'd seen so-and-so lately, he'd say "No". Either from not having it register that he had spoken to them yesterday, or then being such a patholigical liar as he was.

The theatre owner used to say, "Before Doc got so busy a practice he'd come in here nearly every night, pick out a back seat, slump down in it and in five minutes be sound asleep - snoring." Time and time again, they would have to wake him up, because he disturbed the people in the show. That was before I worked for him.

Laveta Brim told me once that Dr. Adams had done a criminal abortion on her sister Lavonne. When Laveta went to Dr. Adams for him to do hers, he told me, "Your friend Laveta Brim is pregnant; and asked me to fix her up". I said, "Well!", and " Are you going to?". He said, "Hell no, I told her she was barking up the wrong tree". I said, "Laveta told me once that you performed an abortion on her sister Lavonne, out in the house, and she screamed so hard you threatened to strike her if she didn't shut up". "Well, that's a Goddam lie", he said," you can go right in the hspital and see her record, where I did a D and C for metorrhagia (or something - he gave some excuse) . She wasn't any more pregnant than I am right now. You can see where the report came back - showing nothing of pregnancy". Well, I got wise to him, or figured I knew what he was doing all the time these D and C's were being done and come back with innocent reports. He would scrape and scrape the uterus until you couldn't get anything else out; then he'd give one final scrape and send that away. Naturally, it would only be uterine mucosa!!!! Quite a system!! For the price I understand was charged; but do not know for sure.

Four

I am almost dead sure, about this system. I am sure he used it.

Right after I started to work for him, Dr. A. said, "After the beating my friend John has given you, Jeff will be good to you". Well, I wasn't interested in Jeff or anybody like him. But he used to visit the Dr. Even at their house I understand. And while he would be in Live Oak, the Dr. would get Mary, and after ten P.M the four of us would go out to Mac's on the Suwannee River, and have a steak as big as a barn. There was no drinking. They would sit there and visit, until Mary and I could have just dropped in our tracks. Mary and I would play "bowling" on one of those machines. And sometimes they would join us. I loathed J.J. Elliott. To me he was just a big fat "biddy". An old lady. I was afraid Dr. Adams might be angry if I was not polite to J.J. And, almost at any cost I had to keep this job. At that time I suppose I had a million fears running through my system; fear of losing another job; fear of people, gossip; and Dr. Adams guaranteed me safety—which - give him credit - he lived up to! He treated me like a long lost baby-sister. The day he hired me I told him I wasn't going to stand for any monkey-business, and I wanted protection because Sims had threatened my life, which I know he will stoutly deny. Dr. Adams said, "You don't have to worry, you've never known protection until you've worked for me. I take care of all my employees, and treat them right". He hired me - not privately; but in front of the staff and at least twenty patients. I was a little embarrassed. He gave you the impression that he never had a thing to hide. Always did things above board. Well, he did, except for those things he did below board!! One night when we were out at Mac's Tavern, we had just arrived; and not 10 minutes later Dr. and Mrs. Sims came in and Mr. and Mrs. Ed. Kent (Their friends). I had only been working for Dr. Adams about a month. Dr. Sims was paralized drunk, but holding it well. He looked like he had been dragged through a pint-sized knot-hole backwards, fifty times. I never felt sorrier for him, than then. I knew why he was so drunk and why he looked so terrible. I had done it. He was dissappointed in my attitude and I suppose, he, too, was afraid, of what I might tell Adams professionally (which was next to nothing), and what Adams could do to him. Believe me when Dr. Adams got on your tail, you were done for. Had he lived five more years, I don't know for sure just how John Sims might have made out. And I'm not kidding. Because, Dr. Adams, DID NOT WANT DR. SIMS AROUND! Well, I looked rather funny, and I guess I looked embarrassed. Dr. Adams," I am sorry, Miss Park, subjecting you to this. It makes it look bad, you with Mr. Elliott. And, they'll never know that it is platonic. If we had known we could have gone to eat in Lake City or someplace". He was as nice as nice could be. I just said, "It's alright". He seemed to have a wonderful acumen, himself. He could spot a situation a mile away; and read your mind like no one's business.
    About a week after I started to work for him, he introduced me to Mary in his wine Olds, in the ambulance drive at the hosp. They were sitting in the fron seat; I was standing on Mary's side of the car. When I shook hands with her (t she hesitated, and I noticed him nudge her, and she held a LIMP hand to be shaken. She wore a thin nylon-voile long-sleeved blouse (white), in which her breasts showe ed up to great advantage, and in the darkness of the drive, with only the indide hospital lights reflecting out, her blonde hair looked fairer than ever, and her blue eyes, bluer than ever, and she had that little mexican dog,"Duchess", and I was highly impressed. Whether she did it for the occas'on, or not, I don't know. Also, her perfume. I forget what it was. But, I though Mary was very beautiful, and graceful. A long time later, she told me, that on that night she didn't know whether to shake hands when I held my hand out, ob ignore it, but that he had nudged her. She said, that she was not looking forward to meeting me, tho' she knew she was bound to, because of the terrible reputation I had in Live Oak. Was I any worse than she? I'd say, at least I'd venture to say, - a lot better. My mother isn't a whore, anyway. Mary told me she was sorry she had taken

Five

tthat attitude, that I turned out to be a real nice person. Oh dear, how many
"asses", (pardon me please), and how many types of asses I had to kiss, for at
least six months after I started working for Dr. Adams. Not because I was working
for him, but the gossip gossip that had gone on while I was working for Dr. Sims.
The way ignorant people can pierce their way into your precious and sacred privacy!!
And make something beautiful, their their dirty damn gossipy business. I was like
Dr. Adams,.... I spoke to every, dirty or clean, Tom, Dick, and Harry, and patted them
on the shoulder, and gave them a kind smile, and laughed and joked with them, while
I was trying to do work, keep Sims and Haskell off my back, and Joy Kimsey, and "Aunt"
Sarah, the dirty wh-----, keep my head up and try to smile all the time, as if nothing
bothered me, while inside I was broken all to pieces and crying dry tears - and NOT
feeling sorry for myself. AND, last, but, not least: try to keep from losing my sane
mind! One month after I started working for Sims, I lost 20 lbs. in two weeks! I
wieghed 145 when I arrived there. I weighed 125 the 15th of January, 1950. 122 to
be exact. I started taking I.V.'s of 50% Glucose (50 cc. daily, into which I had mixed
two ampoules of Lyo-B C (I.V. Vitamins); and Lipo-adrenal cortex ($5.00 a cc.). Nothing
happened for about a month, and my arms were so sore from puncturing them myself.
Then I started gaining, about ½-1 pound a day, and when I got to 135, I only took
it about once a week. I was still taking it when I went to work for Dr. Adams
because to stop meant to lose weight; I had proved that. About a month after
working for Dr. Adams, I stopped entirely, and never needed anything except some
penicillin once in awhile, or some lipo-adrenal cortex if we had a busy siege.
I gained weight easily, and as I have said before, I was never happier.

          He used to tell me that I was a far better anesthetist than Dr. Workman.
Well, I never killed a patient for him, like Dr. Workman did. But, I usually thought
he was filling me with blarney. But, he was gradually working me in to more and more
anesthetics, and Dr. Workman:- out. I don't know if Dr. Workman noticed this or not.
Of course Dr. Workman was doing more surgery himself.

          I guess it was spring of '52 Sam Gibbs came on the hospital board.
Not long after that, Dr. Adams acquired Sam as a patient; but Sam complained to me that
all Dr. Adams ever did was Shoot! Adams stole Gibbs from Sims. Adams stole every patient
he could from Sims. He may have shown much professional ethics to me, and in front
of me; but none to his co-workers, except Workman, and old Price, and Black, because
he could "manage" Black, and somehow or other he respected Counts. I helped him
respect him. Anyway, he knew him before. But, Russell was always good to me, and I
told Dr. Adams not to hurt Dr. Counts (once, when he started to), because Dr. Counts
had always treated me like a queen. I don(t even remember what he was going to do to
Counts, but it was something that Counts and Sims were in together, and in order for
Adams to hurt Sims he had to involve Counts. And, I got mad and told him not too.
And he said he wouldn't; and I said, "And don't do it behind my back, either!" And
he didn't, as far as I know. It was just another little thing around the hospital.
It was just the little things that Adams worked on, and they built up and could break
a person. I know! Sims used the "little-method" psychology on me! I was so scared
when I left him and started to work for Dr. Adams, that one night, when Russell
asked me to go to the Bl. Lge. with him, I left a note, sealed in an envelope
"TO BE OPENED IN CASE OF MY DEATH", stating where I was, who with, and who I suspected
would be behind my death. As, I told you my life was threatened both by Sims and
Haskell. But, this was one night, that Counts had come in from Chattanooga, and said
he wasn't going to show his face in Live Oak until noon the next day, because he wanted
to see me. And, I thought maybe it was something Sims had cooked up, and that Counts
would NEVER show his face in Live Oak, and the others would have alibis, and there I
would be, my dead dead body murdered, and unable to find anyone that did it. Also,
Counts had come to my apartment,; he had NOT telephoned in! While he was waiting in the
car, I had written the note. Needless to say, I got home safely. And, he was only
curious to know if I was happy in my work, and if LeRoy was treating me with kindness.
Russell was confused. He liked peace, and hated this terrible Live Oak strife. He used

MRS WHITFIELD GAVE ME A LOT
OF THEM — BLESS HER HEART

typo's

the lipo-adrenal about twice a week, only.

Six

to say, "It may be Hell's Half Acre, but I am always glad to get back home to the Briar-Patch". That's what he called Branford. Because Live Oak was always just getting ready to erupt, or had just erupted! I told Dr. Adams about going out with Russ., and told him about the note, and why. He said, "You don't have to worry about Russell Counts - he wouldn't harm a hair on your head. He's a nice fellow". Dr. Adams said he would keep it confidential , which I am sure he did. He respected Dr. Counts; I believe he felt inferior to him. He never tried to hurt him. Of course, Adams knew it would gripe Sims if he and Counts could carry on a civil conversation for 20 minutes. He and Sims couldn't say, "Good-morning". Hardly ever did. About 6 months after I was working for Adams, Sims wasn't speaking to me either. Of course, I don't blame him.

He did just enough bad to not get caught; and just enough good to get by. But, he did have my respect as a doctor. Many things I DID NOT like the way he did. Like running his day office work; treating the people like a bunch of cows, instead of sitting down in privacy and talking with them, and discussing their problems, and giving them a thorough examination he'd look at their teeth, and say to Mrs. Wilson, " A cc penicillin; - next patient". And, he'd have three or four patients crowded in one room; some woman trying to get her pants on, and a man having his taken off so he could look at his pylonidal Cyst healing, a child with a runny nose taking it all in, and likely as not some young, teen-ager, pregnant as hell (well 2-3 weeks) waiting to get him alone to ask him to do her a favor. Now, I don't know about the latter for sure; but the more I stand back and look at things, I often wonder. ???

I forget what for; but I guess it was when Mrs. Allen got so pregnant she couldn't work anymore, and he asked me to work in the office too, until he got relief. (Then came Jean Hart). So, I worked for a couple of weeks, I think. Believe me, it was hard work; because I made it hard. I gave those patients a treat. I lined up chairs snug against one another all along that left wall, from his office into where the X-ray was. It took care of about ten patients at a time. And all ten had: (1) Blood pressures checked. (2) Pulse. (3) Temperature. (4) Urinalysis (5) Weight. (6) Complaint that day (7)Onset (8) Every helpful detail was jotted down briefly, for his benefit. Even things they were not complaining about; like someone would come in for "pain in the belly; cramps in the bowels"; I'd notice some unhealed ulcers on their legs (Varicose ulcers; leuetic ulcers?) I made a note of it "Check in case of lues", or anything that would help. He never told me, but Mrs. Wilson told me, He had said, "That Park is a hard woman to beat. I like this system." He would never put his foot down and make the girls do that. He was a poor hand at giving orders. He actually lacked guts to carry out good routines and good systems. That was NOT part of his scheme to get ahead; it was lack of this GUT that made him do all these underhand things!!! There are many filthy rich, prominent men, to-day, that got that way just as hard a s Dr. Adams worked, but, HONESTLY, and with good management principles. He had NO GUTS. I think he w was maybe as scared a person (with lots of bluff) as anyone I have ever known. Even, though he hit the dog on the road. Only Mary and I saw him. We wouldn't hold fists up in his face. He wouldn't have done that if the owner of the dog, and a big husky friend of the dog's owner had been with him instead. We are taught, as you must know, any obesity is caused from overeating. Very little is thought to be "Glandular", as used to be considered. Obesity, from overeating, means a disturbed and unhappy mind! He could eat a steak (all but the bone; fat and all) out at Mac's, in 5 MINUTES! Fried onions, hush puppies and all. And, say, "That tastes like more, doesn't it Jeff?" And Jeff would rave and marvel at how fast he had eaten it, and still wanted more. Often, mornings after surgery, he'd ask me over to the house, and to eat breakfast. "Florrie, I'm here. So's Miss Park; do you think we can feed her? Did that chicken lay any more than two eggs yesterday? You didn't know we had a pet chicken did you Miss Park?" Plenty of scrambled egg was in the oven to keep warm, and toast, and bacon. I would hardly have my fork in mine, and he would have GULPED his up, be barging out the door,"You take Miss Park home, Florrie. I've got to go". He liked his coffee cool; he could drink it faster - in one gulp. This would be about 9:45 A.M.: he would be taking off for the office. "I wish LeRoy wouldn't eat so fast!", Mrs. Adams would say.

Seven

And, as you know, he would eat whatever a patient would offer him. He never said, "No", to candies at the hospital. Grab 4 or 5 in hishand and walk away. Danish Pastry and sweet rolls were nearly always in the front seat of the car. He smoked heavily. Heavier than most people ~~tought~~ thought. He smoked cigars, the aroma of which I love, and fully approve of, and am a good judge of. Mary ca n tell you what he smoked. They may have been expensive, because they smelled very good.

Mary (and Jeff) (and Kieth Black) know more about this than I do: he blew up with dynamite something over in Lake City, where his farm is, making that lake, I think. The guy (other) involved was as mad as hell, and put out financially, I think; but, nothing could be proved. Not with Kieth Black, there I wouldn't think. Whatever it was, it was a dirty trick, and no one with principle or good scruples would have thought of doing it.

At one time I knew the details of it, but they have slipped my mind. I don't see why Mary won't tell you. But, maybe, by now you have seen Mary. I had better get this in the mail.

I feel very inadequate, that I have not given you much; and that I have repeated myself some, in this letter; and that maybe I have dwelt on myself too much. Maybe you would have some questions, that I may be able to answer. Or my memory may serve me better as I try to think deeper (as I am doing, now).

However, for now, I think I'll close, and drive into the P.O. and drop it in to get an early start in the A.M. As I can't get away until noon, due to work.

I have been thinking over the 27th and 28th and how very much I enjoyed them, in spite of being slightly under the weather. You are a magnificent host, and to me your kindness and hospitality knows no bounds. You made me feel very comfortable, and very much at home, and at ease. Too flowery? Take it or leave it; I mean it!

Will close for now, and try to do much better in the future. I am trying to think of what other angles I can "attack" Dr. Adams from, so you can have as clear a picture of it all as I have. Everything is so vivid to me; yet, I don't have the ability to get it all across to you. I am glad my first (or among my first) pieces enabled you to see the man better. What are they called? Hypochondriacs? Schiz.? He could be as kind as kind. He could be as ~~XXXX~~ cruel as cruel. Some of his Kindnesses were from the heart; not part of the scheme. I think (of course this was scheming — I'm not kidding myself or anyone else) when he hired me he felt sorry for me. But, as I worked on for him, I think he fully realized the good deed he had done. Anonymously Yours,

And I think he was glad he had done it.

APPENDIX B:
LETTERS WRITTEN BY RUBY MCCOLLUM

Notes on the Letters

The following are all of the known extant letters written by Ruby McCollum, ranging from early in her trial in 1952 from the Suwannee County Jail to many years later in her confinement at the Florida State Mental Hospital in Chattahoochee. It is quite possible that family members have other letters as McCollum wrote frequently to them as can be seen in her references to family members and their various life events.

When a letter has a date, it is given. Sometimes envelopes were preserved and sometimes they were not. Often, pages are very small, and where numbers are given, they represent page numbers. Original letters are archived in Box 3, folder 274, of the Huie collection at Ohio State University in Columbus.

No attempt was made to correct spelling, grammar or punctuation.

As a matter of background, P. Guy Crews was a former state representative and was a Jacksonville attorney, ambulance chaser and defender of bolita figures across North Florida. He had many political connections. Along with his crony, Cogdill, he collected tens of thousands of dollars from the McCollums. Crews was later suspended from the Florida Bar and a new trial had to be set during jury selection. Cogdill was convicted of mail fraud. At that point, Frank Cannon, the attorney who stayed with Ruby through her trial, came on and was paid about $7,000, of which McCollum demanded most of it back when he lost her case. She then fired him numerous times. Releford McGriff, her black attorney, represented the McCollum estate during probate proceedings until he joined Cannon and Crews on McCollum's appeal to the Florida Supreme Court. Because he was reinstated to the Florida Bar months after McCollum's trial, Crews was asked to join the appeal because of his political connections in Tallahassee.

Early filings in the trial began in August, but the trial proper was not until December. The trial ended a couple of days prior to Christmas, 1952.

The Letters

<u>First Set of Pages:</u>

1) Mr. Crews Buck sent you to defend my case with the help of Mr. Cogdill. So please don't throw me down. Continue to use the defence relationship—six yrs. He is the father of my baby. He let my husband run nos. for my sake. He wanted me to get on the table Aug 3.

2) You read this I am sending you and you be the judge. I have not said anything to Mr. Cogdill. Only told him that I could not go on a note for him nor sign any papers. He will have to wait until I see Buck about the rest of his money. If it is necessary to use insanity in the defence alright. I would like to talk to you. You are the defending lawyer.

3) If you do not want to work with Mr. Cogdill you can get another white lawyer to work with you and Buck can pay him I can talk to him. Why did you change? Please don't let him fool you Mr. Crews. Buck doesn't want him for the main lawyer he wants you. I told him what happened.

4) Buck doesn't want Mr. Cogdill he wants you. And Mr. Cogdill to help you. You get the same chair (seat) back. This man wants me to tell a lie and I am not going to do it. So don't pay him no attention. You ask me some thing in front of him.

5) Anywhere you think it is O.K. to have the trial have it there please sir any place it is best for you to work. Buck said Since Mr. Cogdill was there let him work with you. Please don't pay him any attention Mr. Crews do like Mrs. Maple told you to do, she is looking out for me. This man

6) Doesn't like Mrs. Maple all he wants is my money. That's why he didn't want you or anyone else to talk to me, he was doing me so unfair. He doesn't want this to come out on the Dr. If you run it you will easily run it, because it will be the true happenings. As you were going the people liked it.

Second set of pages:

1) Dr. Adams had given me some protolac and viasineral said I would be crazy as hell in a few months. In May he sent me to Brewster Hospital for treatments, Jan. and March for treatments because of shots he would give me if he got mad. (if I didn't do as he said do) Then I asked him would he kill me for some thing like that? He said yes if I have it to do. After the baby came and after I got pregnant year

2) Before last in Oct. he didn't hardly want me to speak to a man. Oh! Well he was boss Of course I was afraid of him since he started with me over six years ago. When he get mad at me he would tare into me like a lion. Plus give me a big shot of medicine to almost kill me. I ask him for something for it he says I know you are sick. What kind of casket

3) Do you want me to get you? I will be to your funeral. If I don't have my husband to take me to a Dr. or go myself he wouldn't do anything for me until he got ready to. I was afraid to tell another Dr. what he had given me because he would beat me up if he found it out. Especially if it was a Dr. in the county. I ask why would you want

4) To do that way? He said it takes a little of that for you some times I told him I could only see him when my old man is out. He said you can see me any dam time you want to. After the baby came I ask if he would operate on me so I want get that way again he said yes I guess I am too old for that kind of stuff. I said no it isn't that. Then he said I will operate on you, he gave me a needle full of medicine that swole my stomach so large my pressure went up to

5) 156 degrees I went to a Dr. here and told him how I felt he gave me a big shot of pinnicillin and I took some yellow capsules that Dr. Adams had given me for influenze, I was real sick for four days before he called and ask how I was doing? He came out to my house and told me that was the kind of operation I needed. Then I told him please don't let me die, I will do anything any time if I have to get my devorce. So

6) He said the idea of you want to be cut on. Lot of women wish they had the healthy ovaries or organs you have. I am not going to cut you and you bet not have one when I get ready for you to have one I will do it and not before; Then I said O.K. you are the boss. As I stated in the beginning about the protolac it destroyes the organs, makes one ache in the joints give

7) One pneumonia or TB's if it isn't taken out of ones body; In July he gave me two CCs of clear medicine that made my head hurt in the top and my heart ran away. He said I would be all right before morning. I laid down went to sleep and slep about an hour I woke up drunk, crazy, seam as if I would die anyway. I thought of some medicine he had given me. It was two CC of Ioda lake-S that was

8) The only thing eased my head and heart. But I continued to feal foolish in my head. And hurt in my joints. He gave me these shots because I told him if he would give me something to get it out I wouldn't ever ask him to do anything else for me. And by, he turned red (mad) a few min. I told him that I was sorry, but I am sick and don't have anyone to help me with my baby or my two little girls. Then he said if I can't have you I will fix you so no one else can have

9) You. Every morning I wake up aching in my right shoulder. I told the sheriff this [space] As I told you This Sunday morning Aug. 3 I went to him for something to get the pain out of my shoulder. He started to give me procaine pinnicillin in suspension and hystadil I said that's what you are going to give me? He changed and gave me procaine pinncillin G. with Sodium I told him I owe you for two calls this makes me

10) Owe you how much he said $9.00 I gave him $10.00 he gave me $1.00 back. I said I want to pay $100.00 on the $116.00 bill that was sent to Sam he said O.K. Then he said get on the table I said, wait until another time for that he started fussing about his money he shook me, began beating on me, I begged him not to bother me, he said I'm gona kill you grabbed a pistol stuck it in my stomach while tusseling over it it went off when he turned it went off again. He wanted me to get off that table.

11) Dr. McCullagh treated me These are the shots that he gave me then sent me to the hospital. He gave me this 1st April.
Protolac, viasineral, manganease permanganate, thiamine, procine penicillin in suspension, cinagil, panthodrene, pentro extract, thiamine hydrochloride. Yes we have had relations over six years. He is my babys father. This is what I wanted to tell you about. I am not talking to no one. Keep the defence you have going.

<u>Third Set of Pages:</u>

1) Mr. Cogdill was over here Thursday evening aske when had I saw you I said Monday. He said he talked to you Wednesday night and yesterday morning. Then he said he wanted to get my people together if I would give him a note to give Buck. He wants the rest of his money if he can get it. I told Buck wasn't going to pay him all of it now no way. He said you know I can have this thing set up or reversed I didn't say anything. He also something about a phyciatrist. Then he wanted to know if I got along as good here as did in Raiford. I said I don't know.

2) He told Lawyer Blackwell who helped Sam in his no. business etc. That I had a baby for Dr. And gona have another one for him. He had another man with him said his name is Mr. Carson from there, this man said Cogdill is the best Ruby I didn't say anything I just want you to know what's happening. He said the Judge Adams was the only one on his side. Kept saying he needed some money now. So if you need any extra money to get everything going your way let me know.

3) He told me if he could get old Howell out of it he would be alright, he must have been friendly to your husband wasn't he? I said I don't know. He didn't want you or anyone with good since to talk to me. The baby is just like the Dr. Mr. Cogdill had those people putting acid and dope & pills

4) something in my food a week after I got there and gave me a big shot (hypodermic) (Phenonian) the same day I wrote to you I was crazy as the devil, I told her the sheriff told me not to take needles, she said you have one baby for the Dr. and gona have another one. I really didn't know what I was doing when I wrote to you.

5) I told the sheriff about those pills & shot too when he came for me last week. You can let the jurors see her or her picture she is just like him. Of course I didn't take the pills I stop eating for a while until I told Mrs. Rosen how drunk & sick I felt. She told me to get what I wanted cut of the little store at Raiford. This medicine was to make me loose the baby but I threw the pills away, but they didn't know it. Mr. Cogdill told them to give it to me. He said someone told

6) Him that I had one baby for the Dr. and was gona have another one for him. I told him that Dr. Adam's friends relatives and everybody else knew about it it isn't a secret at all. Dr. A. said if they wanted to know anything send them to me. Well you know I didn't hear anything about her until I got in Raiford White & Colored would just play with her and that was all. I would do anything the Dr. told me to do because I was really

7) Afraid of him. He snatched me up to him and hit me five –r six times and said I am tired of so much dam foolishness in the office right before that colored nurse, and the waiting room was full of people white & colored. He would tive me needles to make me sick then give me one to get me well when he get mad at me. Beat me up, that was common. He didn't care who knew it. Where I caught up with Mr. Cogdill, he ask me

8) Some questions and I wouldn't ans. Then, he said I will have to get a phyciatrist. I didn't say anything. Then he said if you get Buck he would come in loud talking everything he says goes, if I get Dr. Hampton he would say if she is crazy why don't you send her to an institution? He knows I am going to tell you the real things that's why he doesn't want you or no one else to talk to me. After you became my lawyer a News Editor from Jaxville Melson he said came in and ask two or three question

9) Is the Dr. your baby's father? I said I don't care to talk. He got sore and said if your layer Cogdill told you not to talk don't talk. Why didn't you keep Mr. Douglas? I said we didn't have his price. My bro-in-law had to hire someone we could pay. He said who is it in your family has since enough to tell you what to say? He said you are the one, smart you are not sick. I said I know what's hurting me. This is my body. He said you wouldn't give me your story don't give it to no one else. I didn't

10) Say anything. He said don't give it to a Colored Editor. Then he left. I just want you to know what's happening. I guess he had them to give me that medicine to make me forget, or be slowing in thinking. He had me off a little but I am doing O.K. now. He also said this Mr. McClain on the gate at Raiford was his Bro-in-law. I think he was his look out man. Dr. Adams said Ruby I will do anything for you, I'll give you anything you want, there is anything too good for me to do

11) For you. He wanted me to get my devorce I said but I Have three children to see after then he said I'm too dam poor I have to work for my living. When I asked for the devorce my husband told me he would kill me & the children then kill hisself before he would give it to me. The Dr. was nice but mean and jeavous, if I didn't do as he said do, he would try to tare me to pieces, And I was just Afraid of him. And tried to do anything he asked me to do

12) Mr. Cogdill was here today (Saturday) saying he wanted to get a phciatrist still asking for money I told him Buck was in the hospital and I couldn't say anything. Can't I ask him to quit? I am tired of him worrying me now. I'd rather to pay him to quit. Every time I look up he is here. I will tell him Buck said quit. I don't believe you need him no way.

8/23/1952 Special Delivery from Raiford

Mr. Crews,

I have not had no relations with the Dr. and no other man but my husband. The Dr. Was not connected in any way with my husband in the numbers. As it is rumored. The Dr. Is not my baby's father. Please come to see me at once. Also Mr. Perkins.

Ruby McCollum

Note: Above letter differs from McCollum's usual syntax.

2/19/1953 From Suwannee County Jail

Mr. Cannon,

I am not able to pay no one else to work for me. Since I am depending on other folks for help they advise me to let them get their choice for a lawyer.
Since I have paid you $4000.00 you can kindly return my $3000.00 check at once, because I really need it to pay my bills. Send your resignation at once. Thanking you for everything good you have done for me.

Very truly,

Ruby McCollum

Note that this is two months after her trial is over in December, 1952, and during the process of filing her appeal with the Supreme Court.

3/4/1953 From Suwannee County Jail

Mr. Crews,

I want to see you at once.

Very truly,

Ruby McCollum

4/17/1953 From Suwannee County Jail

Mr. P. Guy Crews,
Notter St. Jacksonville, Fla

Dear Sir:

Please resign from my case, You and Mr. Cannon are fired for good. I notified the Governor, State Supreme Justice, Judge Adams, and the Sherif of Suwannee County that you were fired over three months ago. I want a refund of my money. $4,700.00.

Very truly,

Ruby McCollum

3/27/1953 from Suwannee County Jail

Mr. Crews,

Please come to see me at once.

Ruby

5/ ?/53 From Suwannee County Jail

Mr. Cannon,

Please send me your resignation at once. And a refund of $3,000.0.

Ruby McCollum

5/5/1953 From Suwannee County Jail

Dear Mr. Crews,

I want to talk with you. Don't bring Mr. Cannon over here. Come at once.

Very truly,

Ruby McCollum

5/27/1953 From Suwannee County Jail

Mr. Cannon,

Please come to see me at once. I forgot to say Dr. Adams is Loretta's father. Also the one I miscarried (erasure) I wanted to ask if I could correct my self in the courtroom but didn't know if I could have or not. Samuel McCollum is my thre oldest children father. Bring Mr. McGriff and Mr. Crews. I just could not think fast today at all.

Very truly,

Ruby McCollum

First sign of Ruby's deterioration in her letter writing and first mention of her not feeling well. The "R" in Ruby is beginning to change shape, but the "Mc" punctuation and the period at the end of her name are the same. Letter to Crews on same date:

Mr. Crews,

The question that was asked about the father of my four children? Samuel is father of my three oldest children. Dr. Adams is Loretta's father (the baby) also father of the one I miscarried.
I wanted to correct myself in the courtroom but I didn't know if I would be permitted. I couldn't think as fast I wanted to. Please come to see me you Mr. Cannon and Mr. McGriff.

Very truly,

Ruby McCollum

6/7/1953 from Suwannee County Jail

Mr. P. Guy Crews.
Mr. Crews,

I want you to come over here now I want to talk to you. You can let Mr. Cannon work with or under you if you want to. It is up to you, but I want to see you at once.

Yours,

Ruby McCollum.

Matthew will let you have some change.

9/27/1953 from Suwannee County Jail

Mr. Cannon,

Please come to see me at once and continue to work on my case.

Ruby

Tell Mr. McGriff to disregard the letter I sent to him Sat. I mailed it through mistake.

11/17/1953 From Suwannee County Jail

Mr. Crews,

Please come to see me at once.

Yours,

Ruby

11/22/1953 from Suwannee County Jail

Dear Mr. Crews,

Buck's wife wants you to get me a new trial as you promised. If you can't say so. I want to see you at once. Some things she told me to ask you. Don't bring Mr. Cannon.

Yours,

Ruby McCollum

[On back:]

She also said she will take care of court expenses. At once come to see me now. She said it isn't right for me to be punished to death about my husband's money.

This is well into the appeal to the Supreme Court, which will result in a re-trial in 1954.

12/08/1953 from Suwannee County Jail

Mr. Cannon, Crews

Your service is no longer needed on my case. Please send me your resignation at once also a refund of my $3000.00

Very truly,

Ruby McCollum

P.S. I'm not loose. To deprive me of my 3 mo. Baby is murder. You promised me a new trial. I have never ran after men for my living. I was happily married. No one knows anything about me except I am Ruby regardless to color. Some one else has my case.

(NOTE THE I AM RUBY REGARDLESS TO COLOR STATEMENT)

Same date, separate mailing:

Mr. Cannon, McGriff

Your service is no longer neede on my case. Please send me your resignation at once. Also a refund of my $3000.00.
I am not loose to be deprived of my 3 mo. Baby isn't anything but murder.

Very truly,

Ruby McCollum

This is for Mr. Crews too. I don't have to run after men for my living.

3/05/1954 from Suwannee County Jail

Dear Mr. Huey,

Regardless to what any one says I still want you to please help me I really need it.
I wrote Mr. Cannon and told him that I did not want him on my case at all I fired him.

Very truly,

Ruby McCollum

LETTER ON SAME DAY:

Dear Mr. Cannon,

I wrote and told you that I did not need or want you on my case at all you know that I told you why.

Yours truly,

Ruby M. McCollum

(NOTE: There is no period after her signature here as there is in all other letters. Also there are differences in handwriting, with the R in her name now developing a loop. It is, however, present in later letters.)

03/08/1954 from Suwannee County jail

Mr. Cannon & McGriff, Will you continue to work on my case?

Ruby M. McCollum

Letter of same date:

Mr. Cannon,

That letter that was mailed to you Tuesday 9th disregard it. I told them not to mail it and they sent it anyway through mistake.
I still can't put you back on my case because my aunt told me to let you stay off my case. For that reason you will have to resign from my case for good.

Ruby McCollum

3/10/1954 from Suwannee County Jail

Mr. Cannon,

To give a woman drugs (medicine) to cause her to miscarry a 3 mo. Baby is murder. I am still expecting a refund of my $3,000.00 your resignation in Dec. 1953. (I sent) I told you Dr. Adams did not have anything to do. With my husband's affairs. I did not ask you to put any trust company over my husband's estate. I did not give no authority to file any papers in the Supreme Court. You are fired off my case for good. That I mean. I did not work for Dr. Adams, I don't know anything about his money or anything else. Dr. Adams was not my husband. I was lawfully married to Sam McCollum it is my priviledge [sic] to say or do anything I want done about the Estate.

Sincerely,

Ruby McCollum

(Note: The probate was actually handled by Releford McGriff, her colored attorney, friend and business partner. He actually saved the bulk of her estate since Sam died in testate and McGriff elected a widow's portion of the estate, the same as each of the 4 children, thus diminishing what anyone could grab. Court costs and Ms. Adams's wrongful death suit later wiped out Ruby's portion so she had to file as unable to pay her legal fees for the appeal and retrial.)

Ruby is also confused in that her appeal was automatic and she did not have to give her consent.)

3/27/1954 from Suwannee County Jail

Mr. Cannon,

Don't send me any more Envelopes addressed to no one nor any papers concerning no one that I want to see. If I want to see anyone. I have hands to write and address them.

Ruby McCollum

I was talking about papers conserning that Estate. I know who I want to see and who I don't to see. Don't mention Mr. Huie to me any more. I am sending him no messages in your typed envelopes. I did not send him any letters in your envelope. Further more you are not on my case and don't send me any thing else in here I told you that I was not going to sign any papers for you I meant that. You are not my lawyer on my case. I have told Mr. Huie the same thing.

3/31/1954 from Suwannee County Jail

Mr. Cannon,

I cant put you back on my case unless I talk with you first.

Yours truly,

Ruby McCollum

Let me see what my aunt says.

Another note on same day:

Mr. Cannon,

I will have to talk with you before I can put you back on my case.

Very truly,

Ruby McCollum

4/03/1954 from Suwannee County Jail

Mr. Cannon, McGriff

You can get back on my case but I want to see both of you at once.

Very truly

Ruby McCollum

Be sure to do as you said you would do. She said it's O.K.

4/09/1954 from Suwannee County Jail

Mr. Cannon,

I still cant put you back on my case. Someone else has it. And you are still fired for good.

Ruby McCollum

P.S. Reasons have been given already.

5/23/1954 from Suwannee County Jail

Dear Mr. Huie,

I am "praying" that you will come in to see me so that I can tell you the whole story.

Very truly,

Ruby McCollum

5/25/1954 from Suwannee County Jail

Dear Mr. Huie,

Please get me a cash bond or have me turned out of this place (free). Please do that as quick as possible.

I am

Ruby McCollum

This is one of the "I am" letters, compare with earlier letter stating "I am Ruby, regardless of color"

8/54 From Suwannee County Jail

Mr. Cannon,

It is my business what I'm gona say,
Don't send no one in here. Don't come in here worrying me any more.

I'm

Ruby McCollum

(Note: **3rd Instance of some variant of "I am Ruby McCollum."**

9/1/1954 From Suwannee County Jail

Dear Mr. Huie,

Please handle my case. I tried those lawyers it is too much confusion between them.

And it is really harmful to me.

I am

Ruby McCollum

[illegible erasure]

(Note: 4ᵗʰ instance of "I am Ruby McCollum")

7/11/1966 from Chattahoochee

Dear Mr. Huie

Please help me. I want to go back home.

Yours truly,

Ruby.

1/27/1969 from Chattahoochee (p 101)

Dear Mr. Huie

Please help me. I want to go back home to my four children.

Yours truly,

Ruby

12/16/1971 from Chattahoochee (page 105)

Dear Mr. Huie,

I have been here since 1954, Sept 16th. This is Dec 16th 1971. I have been up here 17 years. I want to go back to my own home now in Suwannee County.
Please help me.

Best wishes throughout the Holiday.

Yours truly, Ruby.

P.S. all 4 of my kids are married.

December, 1971 From Chattahoochee (page 97)

Christmas card to Huie with "Very Truly, Ruby McCollum"

2/7 date from Chattahoochee (Envelope dated 2/19/1973)

Chatta Hoochee
Florida. 2.7.

Dear Mr. Huie,

I am fealing fair today. I have heard from any of my kids since the holiday. Will you please tell them to write to me (?) (illegible word). Sonya and her daughter were to see me in Dec. I told them to come back for (?) I have not from since. Where have you heard from my lawyers. Hope to hear from you soon. Very truly
I want to go back to my home. Please help. It is my freedom and I want it. I love my Loretta Kay Sonya and Sam Jr. They are my own blood.

(Note: Badly deteriorated handwriting that is hardly legible and missing words as well as overlapping writing making portions illegible.)

5/22/1973 from Chattahoochee (page 108)

Dear Mr. Huie

How are you today. I feal OK, about as well as you could expect. I just want to go back to my Sam Jr, Kay Sonya & Lorettta. I want you to please help me. I was in Live Oak on April, 9ᵗʰ just month. Loretta was not there. I told her to write to you. Hope to see you soon. It is really getting warm here. Plese write Matt and Samuel Jr.

God Bless you

Very truly Ruby,

It is very important

(Note: Writing deteriorated but not as bad as 2/19/1973. Mentions trip to Live Oak. Most likely connected with hearings on release under Baker Act.)

12/16/1973 from Chattahoochee

Hello,

Just to say Merry Christmas and Happy New Year.
Peace on Earth Good Will to Men. Hope to be see you soon.
I'll be loving you always & family (?).
Merry Christmas to all. Happy New Year. God Bless You. Peace on Earth.
Good Will to Men.

(Note: Badly deteriorated handwriting and practically incoherent. Not addressed to anyone but seems to be mailed to Huie with no inside salutation to him.)

APPENDIX C:
DEED TRANSFERRING HOUSE FROM HOPPS TO MCCOLLUM

Original filed in tax records Book 39, pages 318-319 in the Suwannee County Courthouse.

BOOK 39 PAGE 320

TOGETHER with all and singular the tenements, hereditaments and appurtenances thereto belonging, or anywise appertaining and the reversions and remainders, rents, issues and profits thereof, and all the estate, right, title, interest, dower and right of dower, property, possession, claim and demand whatsoever, in law and in equity, of the said part ies of the first part, of, in and to the above-granted premises and every part thereof, with the appurtenances.

TO HAVE AND TO HOLD the above mentioned and described premises, with the appurtenances, to the said part y of the second part, his heirs and assigns, forever; and the said part ies of the first part, and their heirs, the above-described and hereby granted and released premises, and every part and parcel thereof, with the appurtenances, unto the said part y of the second part, his heirs and assigns, against the said part ies of the first part and their heirs, and against all and every person and persons whomsoever, lawfully claiming or to claim the same, or any part thereof, shall and will Warrant, and by these presents Forever Defend.

IN WITNESS WHEREOF, the said part ies of the first part have hereunto set their hand s and seal s the day and year above written.

Signed, sealed and delivered in the presence of

J. W. Bryson   *Jno L. Hopps* (SEAL)

Ella T. Stewart   *Beatrice T. Hopps* (SEAL)

STATE OF FLORIDA,
SUWANNEE COUNTY

I hereby certify that on this day personally appeared before me, an officer duly authorized to administer oaths and take acknowledgments J. L. Hopps and his wife, Beatrice T. Hopps, to me well known to be the person s described in and who executed the foregoing Deed to Samuel McCollum and severally acknowledged before me that they executed the same for the purposes therein expressed; and the said Beatrice T. Hopps , the wife of the said J. L. Hopps, on a separate and private examination, taken and made separately and apart from her said husband, did acknowledge that she made herself a party to said Deed for the purpose of relinquishing and renouncing and conveying all of her right, title and interest, whether dower, homestead or separate property, statutory or equitable, in and to the lands described therein, and that she executed the said Deed freely and voluntarily without any compulsion, constraint, apprehension or fear of or from her said husband.

Witness my hand and official seal at Live Oak, Florida, this day of March,

J. W. Bryson
Notary Public State of Florida at Large
My commission expires Feb. 3, 1946

STATE OF FLORIDA,
SUWANNEE COUNTY

I, J. L. McMullen Clerk of the Circuit Court, in and for said County, hereby certify that the foregoing Deed has been duly recorded in the public records of said County, in Deed Record 39 on page 319-320

Witness my hand and the seal of said Court, this 30th day of March, 19 43

J. L. McMULLEN , Clerk

By *Arthur Brannen* , D. C.

NOTES

[1] Marnie Hughes-Warrington, *Revisionist Histories* (New York: Routledge, 2013), 10.

[2] Nico H. Frijda, "The Laws of Emotion," *American Psychologist* 43, no. 5 (May 1988): 349-58.

[3] Marc C. Carnes, "Shooting (Down) the Past: Historians vs. Hollywood," *Cineaste,* spring 2004, 45-49.

[4] J. K. Rowling, *Harry Potter and the Sorcerer's Stone* (New York: Scholastic, 1998), 213.

[5] Zora Neale Hurston, "The Characteristics of Negro Expression," in *Sweat,* ed. Cheryl Wall (New Brunswick, NJ: Rutgers Univ. Press, 1997), 66. The word was also used by Marjorie Kinnan Rawlings and made official by a resolution of the Florida legislature.

[6] "Mrs. Jernigan Bridge Club Hostess Tuesday," *Suwannee Democrat,* Mar. 14, 1952, Society section.

[7] Dale Wright, "Can Surgery Cure Evil Women?" *Jet,* Aug. 20, 1953, 25-27.

[8] US Women's Bureau, "Women's Earnings as a Percentage of Men's, 1951-2013," infoplease, 2014, www.infoplease.com/ipa/A0193820.html.

[9] US Department of Commerce, *Current Population Reports: Population Characteristics,* Oct. 22, 1953. This and numerous other studies of populations and population characteristics are available at www.census.gov.

[10] Florida Constitution, 1885, http://archive.law.fsu.edu/crc/conhist/1885con.html.

[11] Florida Legislature, "Interposition Resolution by the Florida Legislature in Response to Brown v. Board of Education, 1957, with Handwritten Note by Florida Governor LeRoy Collins," May 2, 1957, World Digital Library, www.wdl.org/en/item/14196/.

[12] Mark Twain, *The Innocents Abroad* (Hartford, CT: American Publishing, 1884), 650.

[13] US Food and Drug Administration, 21 C.F.R. §700.13 "Use of *Mercury Compounds in Cosmetics,* " 2015, www.accessdata.fda.gov/scripts/cdrh/cfdocs/cfcfr/cfrsearch.cfm?fr=700.13.

[14] Yaba Blay, "Dencia Wants to Set the Record Straight on Whitenicious," *Ebony,* Feb. 3, 2014, www.ebony.com/entertainment-culture/dencia-wants-to-set-the-record-straight-on-whitenicious-interview-453#axzz3cQ5vKahb.

[15] World Health Organization, "Mercury in Skin Lightening Products," 2011, www.who.int/ipcs/assessment/public_health/mercury_flyer.pdf.

[16] Era Bell Thompson, "Instant Hair," *Ebony,* Nov. 1965, 139-44.

[17] "Ancient African Look Becomes 'New Look' in Paris," *Ebony,* June 1971, 121-24.

[18] *You Belong to Me: Sex, Race and Murder in the South,* directed by John Cork (Sherman Oaks, CA: Vision Films, 2014).

[19] William Bradford Huie, *Ruby McCollum: Woman in the Suwannee Jail* (New York: Dutton, 1956), 133.

[20] "Final Return, Petition for Order of Distribution and for Discharge of Administrators, Regarding Estate of Samuel McCollum," filed in the Court of the County Judge of Suwannee County, Oct. 1957. Also archived in box 3, folder 274, Huie Collection.

[21] Huie, *Ruby McCollum,* 57.

[22] C. Arthur Ellis Jr., *State of Florida vs. Ruby McCollum, Defendant* (Lutz, FL: Gadfly, 2007), 214-15.

[23] Ibid., 219.

[24] Huie, *Ruby McCollum,* 185.

[25] Ibid., 133.

[26] Ruby McCollum, letter dated Dec. 8, 1953, from Suwannee County Jail, box 8, folder 64, Huie Collection.

[27] Huie, *Ruby McCollum,* 93.

[28] Ibid., 133.

[29] Ibid.

[30] Kerry Segrave, *Lynchings of Women in the United States: The Recorded Cases, 1851-1946* (Jefferson, NC: McFarland, 2010), 5.

[31] Ibid., 119-23.

[32] Ibid., 120.

[33] Ibid., 122.

[34] Mae Clide, "Georgia Brutes Again Lynch U.S. Citizen," *Chicago Defender,* June 29, 1912, 1.

[35] Xcon, "The Shot Doctor," *A Crime to Remember* TV series, season two, 2014.

[36] Huie, *Ruby McCollum,* 78.

[37] Ibid., 85.

[38] Ellis, *State of Florida vs. Ruby McCollum,* 142.

[39] Huie, *Ruby McCollum,* 133.

[40] *Weekly Challenger,* "Was Wealthy Black Woman Driven Crazy to Shoot White Doctor in Head in 1952?" Jan. 3, 2015, http://theweeklychallenger.com/was-wealthy-black-woman-driven-crazy-to-shoot-white-doctor-in-head-in-1952/.

[41] Huie, *Ruby McCollum,* 143.

[42] Ellis, *State of Florida vs. Ruby McCollum,* 65.

[43] Ibid., 82.

[44] Ibid., 87.

[45] Xcon, "The Shot Doctor."

[46] Huie, *Ruby McCollum,* 184-5.

[47] Ibid., 177.

[48] Revenue Act of Oct. 20, 1951, 26 U.S.C. § 3285 et seq. (Supp. 1952), https://books.google.com/books/about/New_Provisions.html?id=fj0iAQAAMAAJ.

[49] Huie, *Ruby McCollum,* 50.

[50] Louie Wadsworth, "Ten Live Oak Negroes Procure Gambling Stamps: 'Bolita Sam' and Crew Sign Up," *Suwannee Democrat,* Jan. 11, 1952, 1.

[51] Louie Wadsworth, "Military Rites Held Here for C. L. Adams III," *Suwannee Democrat,* Feb. 8, 1952, 1.

[52] Huie, *Ruby McCollum,* 156.

[53] Ibid.

[54] Ellis, *State of Florida vs. Ruby McCollum,* 220.

[55] Ibid., 87.

[56] Ibid., 185.

[57] Ibid., 134.

[58] Huie, *Ruby McCollum*, 43.

[59] Ibid., 112.

[60] Zora Hurston, letter to Huie, July 1, 1954, reprinted in Carla Kaplan, ed., *Zora Neale Hurston: A Life in Letters* (New York: Doubleday, 2002), 714-15.

[61] Ibid., 186. See also Edith Park's letters to Huie in appendix A.

[62] Ibid., 187-8.

[63] Huie, *Ruby McCollum*, 188. Also confirmed by Clyde Ellis, the author's father, who worked with Thelma Curry at Suwannee County Hospital after the murder.

[64] Ibid.

[65] Clyde Ellis (author's father), author interview, Live Oak, FL, 1989. Thelma Curry, Adams's office assistant, started work at the Suwannee County Hospital after Adams's death. During a cigarette break, she told Ellis the content of the note on the medical bill.

[66] Ellis, *State of Florida vs. Ruby McCollum*, 285-6.

[67] Ibid. Clyde Ellis was in the operating room when the incident occurred.

[68] Huie, *Ruby McCollum*, 189.

[69] Betty Lou Johnson, author interview, Live Oak, FL, 1965. Johnson, an aunt of the author, was a telephone operator on the switchboard at the time of these calls.

[70] Tammy Evans, *The Silencing of Ruby McCollum: Race, Class and Gender in the South* (Gainesville, FL: University Press of Florida, 2006), xxi.

[71] M. C. Moore, "Psychiatric Evaluation of Ruby McCollum," Sept. 21, 1954, box 3, folder 274, Huie Collection.

[72] Huie, *Ruby McCollum*, 242-3.

[73] Zora Hurston, letter to Huie, Mar. 28, 1954, reprinted in Kaplan, *Zora Neale Hurston*, 704-5.

[74] Zora Hurston, letter to William Nunn, May 28, 1953, reprinted in Kaplan, *Zora Neale Hurston*, 700.

[75] Hurston, letter to Huie, July 1, 1954.

[76] Zora Hurston, letter to Huie, May 14, 1954, reprinted in Kaplan, *Zora Neale Hurston*, 708-11.

[77] Hurston, letter to Huie, July 1, 1954.

[78] Huie, *Ruby McCollum*, 14.

[79] Revella Clay and A. M. Rivera Jr., "Will Ruby Talk," *Pittsburgh Courier*, Sept. 20, 1952.

[80] Ted Poston, "Love and Violence in the South," *New York Post*, Aug. 29, 1954.

[81] *You Belong to Me.*

[82] Ibid.

[83] Huie, *Ruby McCollum*, 133.

[84] *You Belong to Me.*

[85] Ruth Thompson-Miller, *Instructor's Manual and Discussion Guide for Documentary*, You Belong to Me: Sex, Race and Murder in the South (unpublished study guide, n.d.).

[86] Huie, *Ruby McCollum*, 133.

[87] Ibid., 132.

[88] Ibid.

[89] Ibid., 133.

[90] Ibid., 176.

[91] Ibid., 177.

[92] Ibid., 176-7.

[93] Ibid., 177.

[94] Revella Clay, "Insanity Plea Filed for Ruby," *Pittsburgh Courier,* Sept. 27, 1952, 1, 4.

[95] Huie, *Ruby McCollum,* 177.

[96] Hurston, letter to Huie, May 14, 1954.

[97] Zora Hurston, letter to Huie, June 10, 1954, reprinted in Kaplan, *Zora Neale Hurston,* 713.

[98] Hurston, letter to Huie, July 1, 1954, 715.

[99] Huie, *Ruby McCollum,* 93.

[100] Ellis, *State of Florida vs. Ruby McCollum,* 220.

[101] Brad Rogers, interview with William Huie, Lake City, FL, 1982 (private collection, portions reproduced in *You Belong to Me*).

[102] Poston, "Love and Violence in the South."

[103] Trezz W. Anderson, "'I loved Dr. Adams. He Was Not My Enemy,'" *Pittsburgh Courier,* Jan. 31, 1953, 1.

[104] Huie, *Ruby McCollum,* 156.

[105] Ed Morgan, sworn affidavit, Sept. 16, 1954, box 84, folder 84, Huie Collection.

[106] *You Belong to Me.*

[107] Ellis, *State of Florida vs. Ruby McCollum,* 286.

[108] Huie, *Ruby McCollum,* 189-90.

[109] Huie, *Ruby McCollum,* 185.

[110] Ben Green, *Before His Time: The Untold Story of Harry T. Moore, America's First Civil Rights Martyr* (New York: Free Press, 2005), 48-51.

[111] Evans, *The Silencing of Ruby McCollum,* 57.

[112] Hurston, letter to Huie, June 10, 1954.

[113] Evans, *The Silencing of Ruby McCollum,* 57.

[114] McCollum, letter dated Dec. 8, 1953.

[115] Evans, *The Silencing of Ruby McCollum,* 59.

[116] Ibid., 60.

[117] Alice Bullard, "The Truth in Madness: Colonial Doctors and Insane Women in French North Africa," *South Atlantic Review* 66, no. 2 (2001): 115.

[118] Ibid., 114.

[119] Ibid., 118-19.

[120] Andrew Scull, *Madness in Civilization: A Cultural History of Insanity from the Bible to Freud, from the Madhouse to Modern Medicine* (Princeton, NJ: Princeton Univ. Press, 2015), 162.

[121] Ibid., 116.

[122] Ibid., 118.

[123] Evans, *The Silencing of Ruby McCollum,* 61.

[124] Manuel Vallee, "Resisting American Psychiatry: French Opposition to DSM-III, Biological Reductionism, and the Pharmaceutical Ethos," in *Sociology of Diagnosis,* ed. P. J. McGann and David J. Hutson, vol. 12 of *Advances in Medical Sociology* (Bradford, UK: Emerald Group, 2011), 87.

125 Office of the Surgeon General, "Mental Health: Culture, Race, and Ethnicity: A Supplement to Mental Health: A Report of the Surgeon General," Aug. 2001, www.ncbi.nlm.nih.gov/books/NBK44246/?report=printable.

126 Wolfgang Jilek, "Cultural Factors in Psychiatric Disorder" (paper presented at 26th Congress of the World Federation for Mental Health, July, 2001), www.mentalhealth.com/mag1/wolfgang.html.

127 Peter Guarnaccia and Igda Martinez Pincay, "Culture-Specific Diagnoses and Their Relationship to Mood Disorders," National Resource Center for Hispanic Mental Health, 2007, 36, www.nrchmh.org/ResourcesDirectService/Culture-Specific%20Diagnoses%20and%20Their%20Relationship%20to%20Mood%20Disorders.pdf.

128 Renato Alarcón, "Culture, Cultural Factors and Psychiatric Diagnosis: Review and Projections," *World Psychiatry* 8, no. 3 (Oct. 2009): 135.

129 Evans, *The Silencing of Ruby McCollum,* 59.

130 Huie, *Ruby McCollum,* 180.

131 Edith Park, letters and notes to Huie, box 31, folder 27, Huie Collection, reprinted in appendix A.

132 Huie, *Ruby McCollum,* 62.

133 Ibid., 63.

134 Al Lee, "Memory of Murder Fades after 28 Years," *Ocala Star Banner,* Jan. 13, 1980, 1, 2B.

135 Ibid., 61-62.

136 Ibid., 84.

137 *Pittsburgh Courier,* "Ruby's Case: Praise Lawyers' Integrity," May 1, 1954, 1, 5.

138 Ibid., 130-31.

139 Ibid., 63.

140 US Census Bureau, "Current Population Reports: Consumer Income," Series P-60, #15, Apr. 27, 1954. For this and other studies of populations and population characteristics, see the Census Bureau's Web site, www.census.gov.

141 Lee, "Memory of Murder Fades," 1, 2B. Original contract between Huie and McCollum archived in box 32, folder 297, Huie Collection.

142 Ellis, *State of Florida vs. Ruby McCollum,* 250.

143 Ibid., 261-2.

144 Ibid., 287.

145 Ibid. Letter to attorneys written shortly after McCollum's transfer back to Suwannee County Jail, box 3, folder 274, Huie Collection.

146 Ibid. Undated letter to attorneys, box 3, folder 274, Huie Collection.

147 Ibid. Letter to Huie, May 25, 1954, from the Suwannee County Jail, box 2, folder 274, Huie Collection. Also transcribed in appendix B.

148 Evans, *The Silencing of Ruby McCollum,* book cover posted on Amazon, www.amazon.com/Silencing-Ruby-McCollum-Class-Gender/dp/0813029732/ref=sr_1_2?ie=UTF8&qid=1435670314&sr=8-2&keywords=ruby+mccollum.

149 Ruby McCollum, undated letter to attorneys, box 3, folder 274, Huie Collection. Also transcribed as "Third Set of Pages" in appendix B.

150 Ellis, *State of Florida vs. Ruby McCollum,* 285-6.

151 Huie, *Ruby McCollum,* 134-5.

152 Ibid., 66.

[153] Ibid., 16.

[154] Ruby McCollum, undated letter to attorneys, box 3, folder 274, Huie Collection.

[155] Ruby McCollum, letter to Huie, May 23, 1954, box 8, folder 64, Huie Collection. Also transcribed in appendix B.

[156] *Pittsburgh Courier,* "Huie Gets Ruby's Story on Record; Free on Bail: Author Heading for Home," Oct. 23, 1954, 1.

[157] Huie, *Ruby McCollum,* 184-5.

[158] Ruby McCollum, letter to Huie, Sept. 1, 1954, box 8, folder 64, Huie Collection. Also transcribed in appendix B.

[159] Moore, "Psychiatric Evaluation."

[160] Evans, *The Silencing of Ruby McCollum,* 55.

[161] Huie, *Ruby McCollum,* 218-19.

[162] Ibid., 217.

[163] Ibid., 220.

[164] Huie, *Ruby McCollum,* 207.

[165] McGriff had nearly died from a chest wound from his own gun, reportedly fired accidentally when he was cleaning it in his office on Friday, March 5, 1954. *Pittsburgh Courier,* "Probe Shooting of Ruby's Lawyer: Shooting Called Accident," Mar. 6, 1954, 1. Aside from being fortunate for McGriff as well as for McCollum's defense, his survival spared the public yet another conspiracy theory. Despite the inevitable rumors of a suicide attempt, this was never confirmed.

[166] Ibid., 218.

[167] Barbara Schildkrout, *Masquerading Symptoms: Uncovering Physical Illnesses that Present as Psychological Problems* (Hoboken, NJ: Wiley, 2014).

[168] Ruby McCollum, early undated letters to attorneys, written from Suwannee County Jail, box 3, folder 274, Huie Collection. Transcribed in this work in appendix B.

[169] Ellis, *State of Florida vs. Ruby McCollum,* 292.

[170] Keith Boesen, director Arizona Poison and Drug Information Center, e-mail to author, Apr. 23, 2015.

[171] McCollum, early undated letters to attorneys.

[172] W. P. Kennedy, "The Nocebo Reaction," *Medical World* 95 (1961): 203-5.

[173] Sundarajaran Rajagopal, "The Nocebo Effect," 2007, http://priory.com/medicine/Nocebo.htm.

[174] Huie, *Ruby McCollum,* 156.

[175] Thompson-Miller, *Instructor's Manual.*

[176] McCollum, early undated letter to attorneys.

[177] Ibid.

[178] *You Belong to Me.*

[179] Jeffrey Lehman, Shirelle Phelps, eds., *West's Encyclopedia of American Law,* 2nd ed. (Farmington Hills, MI: Gale Group, 2008).

[180] Xcon, "The Shot Doctor."

[181] *You Belong to Me.*

[182] *You Belong to Me.*

[183] *Suwannee Democrat,* "Slaughter Defeats Black by Big Vote for State Attorney," May 9, 1952, 1.

[184] B. J. Mawhinney, director, Retirement System, Office of the Comptroller, State of Florida, letter to Huie, Sept. 16, 1954.

[185] Lee, "Memory of Murder Fades," 1, 2B.

[186] Hurston, letter to Huie, July 28, 1954.

[187] John A. Diaz, "Woman Chased by Mob After Slaying Doctor: Murder of White Medico Touches Off Powder Keg," *Pittsburgh Courier,* Aug. 16, 1952, 1.

[188] Jude Hagin, e-mail to author, Dec. 21, 2014.

[189] Evans, *The Silencing of Ruby McCollum,* 132.

[190] Betty Shannon, program administrator, Records Amendment Section, Florida Bureau of Vital Statistics, e-mail to author, May 14, 2015.

[191] Evans, *The Silencing of Ruby McCollum,* 133-4.

[192] Ibid., 132.

[193] Ibid., 134.

[194] Ibid., 3.

[195] Huie, *Ruby McCollum,* 99.

[196] Hurston, "The Life Story of Mrs. Ruby J. McCollum!" *Pittsburgh Courier,* Feb. 28, 1953, 1.

[197] Eric Musgrove, Office of the Clerk of the County Court, Suwannee County, e-mail to author, June 1, 2015. Musgrove also recounted the evidence from the trial that is still of record in his office, including the bullets from the gun, and a version of the trial transcript that was not transcribed from the wire recording. He stated that the gun used by McCollum is now in the possession of the son of the clerk of the circuit court who was in office during the trial. The gun may be seen in the documentary film *You Belong to Me.*

Made in the USA
Columbia, SC
02 July 2023